Understanding Emotional Intelligence

Strategies for boosting your EQ and using it in the workplace

NEILSON KITE AND FRANCES KAY

KoganPage

LONDON PHILADELPHIA NEW DELHI

First published in Great Britain and the United States in 2012 by Kogan Page Limited

Apart from any fair dealing for the purposes of research or private study, or criticism or review, as permitted under the Copyright, Designs and Patents Act 1988, this publication may only be reproduced, stored or transmitted, in any form or by any means, with the prior permission in writing of the publishers, or in the case of reprographic reproduction in accordance with the terms and licences issued by the CLA. Enquiries concerning reproduction outside these terms should be sent to the publishers at the undermentioned addresses:

120 Pentonville Road	1518 Walnut Street, Suite 1100	4737/23 Ansari Road
London N1 9JN	Philadelphia PA 19102	Daryaganj
United Kingdom	USA	New Delhi 110002
www.koganpage.com		India

© Neilson Kite and Frances Kay, 2012

The rights of Neilson Kite and Frances Kay to be identified as the authors of this work have been asserted by them in accordance with the Copyright, Designs and Patents Act 1988.

ISBN   978 0 7494 5880 5
E-ISBN   978 0 7494 5937 6

British Library Cataloguing-in-Publication Data

A CIP record for this book is available from the British Library.

Library of Congress Cataloging-in-Publication Data

Kay, Frances, 1949–
    Understanding emotional intelligence : strategies for boosting your EQ and using it in the workplace / Neilson Kite, Frances Kay.
        p. cm.
    Includes index.
    ISBN 978-0-7494-5880-5 – ISBN 978-0-7494-5937-6   1. Emotional intelligence.
2. Management–Psychological aspects.   3. Personnel management–Psychological aspects.   I. Kite, Neilson.   II. Title.
    BF576.K39 2011
    152.4–dc22   2011017032

Typeset by Graphicraft Limited, Hong Kong
Printed and bound in India by Replika Press Pvt Ltd

Contents

About the authors

Neilson Kite is a management coach, mentor and consultant on business related topics and a regular speaker at national and international conferences on management, marketing and communications topics. He has been frequently published in the media and has undertaken groundbreaking work for the UN's International Trade Centre and the European Union on business-related projects. A director of a number of knowledge-based organizations and a consultant to high growth businesses, he was previously a teacher of English in the United Kingdom, East Africa and Sweden. He is currently a guest lecturer and mentor at the University of Gloucestershire's business school and specializes in demystifying the issues and jargon that so often afflict academic and corporate life.

Frances Kay acts as a consultant to specialist firms, assisting them in establishing and developing corporate networks and relationships for their business development. With many years' work experience covering politics, the diplomatic service and law, the majority of her time is now spent writing, researching, editing and giving talks based on her book topics. With 25 books published to date, her area of expertise is career management and self development. Frances is editor of *The Good Non Retirement Guide 2011*, and the author of *Successful Networking*, also published by Kogan Page.

They are the authors of *Understanding NLP*, also published by Kogan Page.

Introduction

The purpose of this book is to make the principles and practice of emotional intelligence more accessible to more people in the working environment. It is to help anyone who wants to improve the quality of his or her decision making. It is also to help improve the effectiveness of personal and managerial action. Although mainly focused on work performance, it applies equally well to other relationships and situations encountered outside work.

Understanding Emotional Intelligence is not specifically concerned so much with the detailed psychological theories of emotional intelligence as the application of that psychology to everyday circumstances. There is already a significant body of available literature that explores the physiology and debates the psychology of emotions in greater detail. We are seeking to illustrate the practical choices, decisions and outcomes of emotionally intelligent actions in an everyday and familiar context.

It's all about outcomes

Emotional intelligence provides an approach to situations and events that displaces a natural or emotional inclination with one that will lead to a better outcome. It harnesses a combination of intellect and emotional awareness to produce a better result than either would have done on its own. It also refers to the ability to recognize what we and others may be feeling. This enables us to manage ourselves and our relationships better and be motivated to do so.

In this regard it is a more reliable indicator of likely success than what has traditionally been measured as 'IQ' or 'Intelligence Quotient'. The emotional intelligence equivalent is now commonly referred to as 'EQ' (Emotional Intelligence Quotient).

Through having a better understanding of emotional intelligence and the way EQ can be applied, you will be able to contemplate objectively the relative value of different options that are available to you. More importantly, you will make decisions that consistently lead to more positive and successful outcomes.

A study of 44 Fortune 500 companies by Hay McBer showed that high EQ salespeople produce twice as much income as the average performer. Computer programmers in the top 10 per cent of EQ competency are also said to be able to develop software three times faster. When revisited 40 years after PhD graduation, those who were good communicators and socially competent turned out to have done significantly better in their careers than those who had poorer interpersonal skills.

In every instance where role effectiveness is measured, those with better-developed emotional intelligence consistently perform better. It is important to note, however, that in some situations, a lower EQ need not be inferior to high EQ. Low EQ does not mean failure. There is, however, a correlation between those who fail and their lower EQ rating.

Emotions in the working environment

Emotions have taught mankind to reason.

VAUVENARGUES

How often have you heard people say 'I've not said anything for the moment, but if she speaks to me like that again, she's going to get a piece of my mind'?

Because so much of our life is spent working and we consistently have to interact with people not necessarily of our choosing, it is inevitable that there will be from time to time friction, trauma and spilled emotions.

The emotions we feel are more to do with stress than danger, hurt by criticism more than physical harm and indignation more than physical anger. At least we hope that is the case in our civilized society. We may have been told when young that 'sticks and stones may break my bones but names can never hurt me', but that does not make it any easier to cope with other people's attitudes or behaviour.

In responding to situations, more than anything else it is about how you *control your emotions more than they control you*, and how you use an emotional framework when making choices and decisions, with or without other people.

Typically, one of the most common emotional conditions at work is stress. This may be caused by a mismatch between the perceived demands placed on you and your perceived ability to cope. The key words here are 'perceived' and 'mismatched'.

Why worry about what others think?

Quite often, the anxiety is about what others will think or say about you if you fail, it is not necessarily to do directly with the task in hand. If it happens that it is the task that *is* the issue and you genuinely do not have the resources, be they time, knowledge, skills and help, to achieve the desired outcome, then maybe the task should not have been embarked upon without having first sorted that out. (Was it emotionally intelligent to take it on in the first place?) Alternatively, there needs to be a different strategy to achieve success or to fail without dishonour and recrimination.

Research shows that the vast majority of people *leave their jobs because of their boss*. Many bosses were promoted to their job without having any training in leadership or management and believe their position confers on them automatic wisdom and intelligence – sadly the cause of poor performance that might otherwise have been avoided.

Common areas of stress

There are also some occupations that are well known for being the cause of stress.

In the development of computer systems, for example, there is no point in promising a completion deadline that you are not certain of delivering against because of the 'unforeseens' that will inevitably occur. By comparison, Christopher Columbus, when setting sail for the Americas, had no idea how long it would take, how much would be needed in the way of ship's rations, what obstacles he would find on his way or what he would find if and when he arrived. If he had been asked to provide a timetable and cost–benefit justification to his masters before setting sail, he might never have started.

Stress in such occupations as systems development, if you are a supplier of such systems, is caused by the purchaser's expectations (quite understandably) of the delivery date being the supplier's problem. The supplier feels obliged to compromise between what he knows his customer wants or needs to hear and the reality of systems development being a pioneering process. This is why, in the case of so many very large public sector systems-procurement projects, they fail to deliver against expectations because insufficient contingencies and controls were built realistically into the process from the start.

Unrealistic expectations?

People working in such development teams will feel the stress of their employers' needs to make a profit, the customers' *sometimes unrealistic expectations*, the pressure on their domestic lives and the need to safeguard their reputations as competent workers – a mismatch between demands and perceived ability to cope.

In such circumstances, developers will usually work less rather than more efficiently, will be more prone to make mistakes or overlook important details and are at greater risk of being absent through stress-induced illness. The impact on the project is that it will suffer.

Where does emotional intelligence fit into this quite common scenario?

Should you always do 'the right thing'?

There is often a conflict between being seen to be doing the right thing and doing what might not be obvious but will produce a better final outcome. Purchasers have to be seen to be doing their jobs and are motivated to fit in with what their masters would see as good performance. That might include both budget and timescale as both are concrete and finite. The supplier might be nervous about these but knows that if the requirement is acceded to, someone else might get the business. To counteract this, some suppliers have been known to say that they will sign the deal first and then renegotiate the conditions. The emotionally intelligent approach would be to reach a genuine understanding through getting emotions out on the table and then using the logic of the situation to shift both parties to a common understanding. In that way, the outcome is *much more likely to match expectations*.

Otherwise, both parties will not only be battling with the other's emotions but their own as well.

EQ can be measured and improved

A particularly important aspect of emotional intelligence is how to test it and how to know that it has been effectively applied. Over recent years, psychologists have devised tests to measure how people would be likely to perform in certain roles. These have been used as a basis of selection both in academic pursuits and in assessing suitability for jobs. Until comparatively recently, much of this testing had been based on raw intelligence (IQ), specific knowledge or demonstrable skills and aptitudes. With the emergence of the concept of emotional intelligence, an expression first coined by Peter Salovey and John D Mayer in a 1990 paper, there is now a much better and completely acceptable means of anticipating how people are likely to perform in a future role.

EQ applies to people *and* organizations

However, more than just being useful in the assessment and selection of people, emotional intelligence can be applied to a very wide spectrum of decisions that organizations make. These could include the development of a winning culture and organizational climate, the spread of successful behaviour, improvement of performance and well-being among leaders, managers, employees, customers and suppliers and, ultimately, an impact on society at large.

Although new as an area of study and in its formative years in terms of universally accepted psychological application, emotional intelligence has, by any other name, been around for a very long time. History, literature and religion are full of illustrations that demonstrate both wise and foolish decisions. The reasons for those decisions invariably have an emotional context. If we understand how much those decisions were influenced by emotion and how much by reason we will have a good insight into the reasons for the success or otherwise of our forebears.

We all have to make decisions that affect us and affect others. They can be trivial or have a wide-reaching impact. A better understanding of emotional intelligence, and developing the emotional competencies to improve the results we achieve, will contribute immeasurably to our effectiveness as people. It will also enhance the success of our organizations.

Chapter 01
Emotional intelligence explained and illustrated

Every word you say, every decision you make and every action you take will have some kind of emotional impact. This is true whether you intended it or not and the impact could be both on yourself and other people.

Just the simple act of lighting a cigarette or choosing a chocolate from a box will trigger a set of complex emotions or sentiments in the person doing it and in those who witness it. The emotional response could be positive or negative, pleased, sad, strong or weak, inconsequential, supportive or could sometimes even be one of disgust.

Emotionally intelligent?

'Security processes **MUST** be observed!

This e-mail applies to **YOU**!

Will you **ALL** please confirm your details'

In the same way, in a work environment, the use of something as simple as capital letters in an e-mail, memo or letter requesting a change in process or behaviour, although intended for emphasis, may be construed differently. The use of the device could be seen as adding clarity, pointing the finger of blame, being rude, indicating a poor grasp of grammar or just being helpful – depending on both the sender's and recipient's view of that piece of communication. We all know of examples where, for example, an e-mail has been sent round with the same form of words and content that is neutral to some yet serves only to enrage others.

Wise or unwise?

At a different level, the decision to sell a proportion of a company's stock to a competitor could be seen as wise, rash, impetuous, cunning, too early, too late, just in time, exciting or simply unnecessary. In each case, emotion as well as reason would have contributed to the different reaction.

The challenge to our emotional intelligence is to steer a path through all the possible reactions to arrive at a position where the best outcome has been achieved. Inevitably, this will be harder than acting on face value but will be the basis for a better result.

The variable basis of our judgements

Our 'emotional' judgement depends on our goals, values, beliefs, sometimes prejudices, and previous experiences. There are also more basic emotional responses, such as anger, fear, envy, happiness, sorrow and pride that could occur spontaneously unless we have anticipated them and been able to exercise some degree of self-management. It is said that it takes six seconds to control an angry reaction, six seconds to create empathetic thoughts and six seconds to effect a change. This goes back to our basic physiology and the nervous system's 'fight or flight' mechanism, among others, that reflects our natural instinct for survival, acquisition and reproduction.

What we share with dinosaurs

Central to our primal reactions is a small part of the lower brain called the amygdala. It is positioned close to our brain stems and spinal cords and triggers our emotional and immediate physical reaction. Even dinosaurs had an amygdala. Human beings, as the highest of the animal species, have developed various layers above that and both intellectual and emotional intelligence come from these higher layers.

We have developed infinitely more ways to react than lower animals. Due to learning, experience, personality and other conditions, every human being will respond in an entirely individual way.

Although we depend on reason and judgement in making what we see as being an intelligent decision or taking an appropriate action, intelligence alone is not necessarily enough to create the right effect or to ensure a successful outcome. Intelligence, as measured by IQ has been the benchmark for predicting how someone, or a group of people, will perform in life and in their chosen role or occupation. However, it is now no longer on its own seen as a sufficiently predictive indicator of competency.

Emotional intelligence can be developed

Knowing when to follow our own and others' feelings and emotions, and when to ignore them, is a valuable attribute. Unlike IQ, whose level remains more or less constant throughout life, EQ can be improved through observation, learning and experience. Behaviour is significantly more affected by emotions than just by intelligence.

Emotional intelligence is related to outcomes and informs our choices and decisions. For the very reason that it involves some sort of choice, for every decision there will be a reaction – our own and what we feel about that decision, and in others and what they feel. It can be compared to a game of tennis where we have a choice of ways in which we can play our opponent. Through the experience of playing against them we can develop winning strategies. Although pure intelligence can be applied, it is emotions such as self-belief, confidence and determination to succeed that drive the way we play. To quote Charles Darwin, 'it is not the strongest of the species who survive, nor the most intelligent, but those who are most adaptive to change'.

IQ is not enough

Intelligent actions are now seen to result from a harmonious blend of emotion as well as reason. Reasoning, on its own, is not enough to produce consistent success. Emotional intelligence is about the choices available to people or groups of people. It is about the decisions they make and the achievement of the most favourable outcomes for those involved or affected.

Where it comes from

Emotional intelligence as a discrete area of study came into prominence in the mid 1990s. Daniel Goleman's seminal, painstakingly prepared book, *Emotional Intelligence* served to both crystallize and evangelize what, at the time, was an academic topic. This topic had, during the preceding decade, been the preserve mainly of psychologists and therapists. His work had been influenced by, notably among many others, Peter Salovey and John Mayer. They had in 1990 published a groundbreaking article and coined the expression 'Emotional Intelligence'. The impact of this compelling article put the subject well and truly on the map.

High IQ is no guarantee of success

Their premise for emotional intelligence was that intelligence alone is not a predetermined feature of success in life and work.

Intelligence as represented by IQ ignores aspects of personality, emotion and behaviour that are equally, if not more likely, to show how someone will perform.

Emotional intelligence is therefore an important factor in evaluating people for roles, in making personal and business decisions, reacting collectively to circumstances and also in leading others.

Understanding emotional intelligence will help self-awareness, self-development, and a better understanding of humankind (despite their conscious or subconscious attempts to hide things). This will extend into corporate decision-making and can even have an impact on war, politics and religion.

Great leaders have great EQ

Many of the world's great business and political leaders provide examples of high emotional intelligence as well as intellectual capability. Leaders who have failed have often done so because they were too arrogant or short-sighted to adapt to changing circumstances. Possibly they ignored the fact that autocracy can never be as ultimately effective as social cohesion.

As well as in leadership and management, emotional intelligence is relevant at all functional and operational levels in an organization. As an example, these could include:

- HR departments in the selection, management and development of people;
- marketing specialists in their representations to customers and others;
- accountants in planning and in their handling of difficult financial challenges;
- service departments in their dealings with customers;
- sales departments in their approaches to acquiring and satisfying customers;
- production departments in their handling of labour and assets;

- company owners in their business decisions and leadership roles;
- managers in handling people, activities, resources and communication.

Choices and decisions

This book is complementary to Kogan Page's *Understanding NLP*, first published in May 2009. Whereas NLP (Neuro-Linguistic Programming) enables the decoding and interpretation of language and behaviour, emotional intelligence can be said to focus more specifically on outcomes. In simple terms, NLP shows you what can be done and how to do it, while emotional intelligence enables you directly to exercise choices and make decisions that lead to a desired result.

Your response is up to you

In the popularization of emotional intelligence there have been many instances where the psychology has been 'bent' to accommodate additional ideas that have nothing to do with choices, decisions or outcomes. In some quarters these have been called mixed models of emotional intelligence. This book is intended not to popularize but to make the subject more accessible. The purpose is therefore to inform regarding the development and use of emotional intelligence in the day-to-day situations that people encounter in the workplace. This book also aims to help readers exercise intelligent choice in all aspects of their lives.

Things we cannot agree on

Various definitions of emotional intelligence have been postulated and it has been difficult to pin down one that is definitive. This is mainly because, although we may have a relatively clear view of what is meant by cognitive intelligence, psychologists find it almost impossible to reach a consensus on a definition of 'emotion'.

Our preferred definition is a form of intelligence 'that displaces a natural or emotional inclination with one that will lead to a better outcome'. It presupposes that we are aware of and have control over our emotions, are aware of the emotions of others, can apply influence to others' emotions and use this emotional capacity to achieve success.

It is not simply about us but others too.

How many types of intelligence do we have?

Emotional intelligence is immediately distinguishable from what is known as cognitive intelligence or being 'brainy'. Insofar as cognitive intelligence is measured by such factors as memory or problem solving as used in conventional IQ and other intelligence tests, it is relatively easier to apply a structure and therefore sound metrics. Where emotional intelligence is concerned it would not be practicable to measure the fear, excitement, confidence, worry and so on, that would have an impact on any given situation or event.

Can we measure our innate feelings?

The only means available are either physical sensors, for example to detect changes in heart rate, breathing and other bodily signs, or self-evidence on how people feel at a particular point in time. In the former case, the data are insufficiently granular to produce completely reliable cause and effect conclusions. In the latter, one is depending on subjectivity rather than objective evidence. Nor could we ignore personality factors such as extroversion, introversion, approachability, receptivity to ideas, emotionality and conscientiousness. Emotional intelligence is also tied up with physiological as well as psychological factors where the unconscious and not just the conscious mind are in play.

In addition to cognitive and emotional intelligence, there are various other categories that have a bearing on people's competencies. These are illustrated in Howard Gardner's multiple intelligence theory model that includes:

- words and language;
- logic and numbers;
- music, sound and rhythm;
- body movement control;
- images and space;
- other people's feelings;
- self-awareness.

Emotional intelligence is not a virtue but a component

It is perfectly possible to be successful with low emotional intelligence provided that other forms of intelligence are being applied to a greater or lesser degree. For example, competence in logic and numbers would adequately compensate for a lack of emotional intelligence where someone was fulfilling a number-crunching role. Traditionally such roles require little or infrequent human interaction. A superb orchestral musician would not necessarily need competence in logic and numbers, nor emotional intelligence if he or she possessed sufficient musical intelligence.

Many successful people lack EQ

It can sometimes suit the populist view and commercial promoters to regard low emotional intelligence as failure when it is nothing of the kind. Nor is it necessarily an indicator that someone will or will not be suitable for a particular job or role. Common sense should always override the mechanistic findings of a man-made EQ test.

Having said that, higher emotional intelligence can be regarded as a bonus from which other benefits can accrue. So the superb musician might gain more and better engagements if his or her interpersonal perception were better developed and his influencing skills could be brought to bear on colleagues and other contacts. The 'number cruncher' might also embark on a musical career. A good athlete might well be able to become a good dancer – as seen in recent television shows.

A famous EQ illustration

Known as 'the marshmallow studies', research conducted by Stanford University involved a class of four-year-olds. They were asked to remain in a room while the researcher went out for a period of time. The children were given a marshmallow each and asked to wait. If they resisted the temptation to eat it, they would be rewarded with a second marshmallow on the researcher's return. Some children were able to resist and some were not.

The researchers located the children 10 years after that experiment and found that those who had resisted the temptation to eat the lone marshmallow (in favour of being rewarded with two) had achieved a significantly higher SAT score (+210 points).

This, it was considered, demonstrated the higher innate emotional intelligence in those that had waited.

In two minds

There are times when emotion overrides the rational mind. Even mild-mannered people will make aggressive gestures when riled by another motorist who has done something dangerous or stupid. Although such a response may be out of character, the balance between rationality and emotion has been disturbed by an impulsive reaction rather than considered thought process. As mentioned previously, there is a school of thought that it takes six seconds to bring an impulse under control.

Emotional intelligence presupposes that we all have two minds and that the best results come from a balance between them. Thus we use our emotions positively and take full account of the logic as well as the feelings about the situation. In this way we will achieve the optimum outcome. Different people will have different sets of characteristics and therefore different weightings to that balance but will perform best when that balance is maintained.

Why is emotional intelligence important?

In a competitive world, organizations want to recruit, retain and develop the best talent that they can. At a personal level, people want what is best for them, their families, peer groups and others who populate their social and working lives. The rapid recognition of emotional intelligence as a means of identifying better performers than the norm has led to 75 per cent of Fortune 500 companies using EQ criteria as a means of identifying future high-performing individuals.

EQ can lead to better results

More significantly, if they are based on emotionally sound, intelligent thinking, the quality of decision making in all aspects of life and work will inevitably improve the quality of the environment in which we all exist. As emotional intelligence is linked with outcomes, any improvement in the use of that intelligence will lead to better work/life results for anyone who consciously applies it.

Important emotional intelligence milestones are the publication of Howard Gardner's *Frames of Mind* in 1983, Salovey and Mayer's widely published article 'Emotional Intelligence' in 1990 and Daniel Goleman's definitive early books, *Emotional Intelligence* in 1995 and *Working with Emotional Intelligence* in 1998.

Chapter 02
Emotional intelligence building blocks

The use of emotional intelligence is conditioned by a variety of factors each of which will have a bearing on the decisions made and outcomes achieved. These include personality type, learning and experience, goals, values, beliefs and prejudices, raw intelligence and emotional competency. Although decisions seem to be made spontaneously at times, they will have been affected by a unique 'map' of the process that everyone possesses.

If we think of emotional intelligence as part of a journey to an outcome, we can more easily take account of what happens along the way.

EQ provides a route to better outcomes

The diagram in Figure 2.1 is designed to provide a simplified representation of what that journey might look like and shows the conditioning factors and aptitudes that feed into an emotionally intelligent decision and, one hopes, a desired outcome.

As an evolving area of study, emotional intelligence will inevitably raise debates about definitions used and the different impact and relevance of contributory factors. Be that as it may, the diagram's purpose is to stimulate thought and understanding and provide a structure that will be straightforward and accessible to everyone who operates and makes decisions in a working environment.

FIGURE 2.1   The cycle of an emotionally intelligent decision-making process

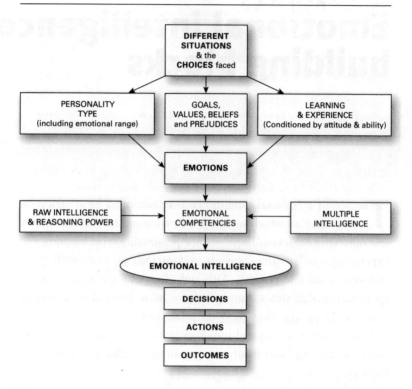

Having created this overall 'picture' each of the boxes will then be opened up into a further representation of constituent parts.

EQ development has a clear and logical narrative

The 'story of the journey' above is that we are all faced, whether as individuals, teams or other organizational or management groups, with situations about which we will need or want to take action. In doing so, we usually face two or more choices as to what to do or say.

Depending on who we are as individuals, or the dominant characteristics of a group, we will tend to apply both intellectual thought as well as some of our emotions in the process. These will have been conditioned by our emotional range, which could be from matter-of-fact to volatile, and by the extent to which attitudes and aptitudes for positive learning have been an important part of our development.

The types of people we are and the actual experiences of our life, flavoured by our ambitions, beliefs and values (and of course prejudices) will feed into our emotional response. This in turn will be modified by our intelligence and the extent to which we understand our own and others' feelings.

Taking all this into account – a subconscious process for the most part – we will apply what now amounts to emotional intelligence in reaching our decision about what action, or not, to take in the circumstances and will know the result we would like.

Dealing with typical situations and your available choices for action

FIGURE 2.2 Typical workplace situations

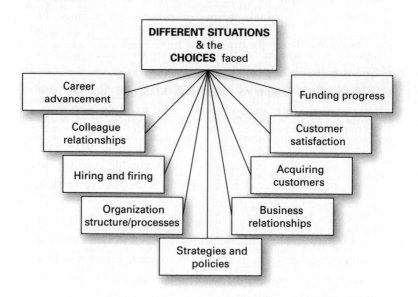

The situations we face could vary from trivial to life-changing but nonetheless will present us with choices. In working life, it is most commonly our interaction with other people that causes us to do or change something. Most problems in the workplace arise because of people and not things. For example, the reason why the vast majority of people change jobs is their wish to get away from others at work – usually poor managers.

How organizations can develop their collective EQ

On a different plane, whole organizations face situations due to political, economic, social and other factors that will affect their fortunes and those of their employees.

At whatever level there is at least a binary decision to be made – to do something or to do nothing. Each has its consequences. You could argue that doing nothing is the easier of the decisions. The reason for this is that if you decide to do something you will be faced with a greater array of choices. On the other hand, you could also argue that doing nothing now leads to a further situation that could be much more difficult to address. It would be more emotionally intelligent to sort out the future today, not tomorrow.

Is 'do it now' always the best strategy?

The topic of many a biblical sermon against excess, often misused, is 'Eat, drink and be merry, for tomorrow you die.' It may be a charming and attractive philosophy for the hedonist but often leads, as has been shown in modern society, to the very outcome that people want to ignore. The proper consideration of future consequences of decisions and actions underpins emotionally intelligent action.

Conventional decisions faced in a business context are generally to do with money, goods or services, people and customers. At a personal level they are about progress, security, recognition, reward and relationships.

There is no situation or circumstance faced that is completely free of any emotional implications. Emotional intelligence, therefore, can always be applied.

Conditioning factors that affect your emotional make-up

FIGURE 2.3 The factors that most influence the way someone will initially react

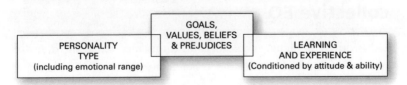

| PERSONALITY TYPE (including emotional range) | GOALS, VALUES, BELIEFS & PREJUDICES | LEARNING AND EXPERIENCE (Conditioned by attitude & ability) |

Personality type

There have been many theories about personality (sometimes referred to as temperament) over the centuries. One of the most convenient and easiest ways to consider personality characteristics is the 'Five Factor Model'. It is also very usable as it is available in the public domain.

The five factors can have both positive and negative connotations but for the purposes of analysing emotional intelligence should be considered just as 'states' and not superior or inferior conditions.

There's nothing wrong with your personality

As is widely understood, a graphic equalizer on a music system enables the optimum blend of tone and volume depending on the type of music being played. In the same way, what one might call a 'personality equalizer' allows for different permutations and intensity of characteristics that match individuals to different roles.

The Five Factor Model includes:

1 Extroversion;

2 Agreeableness;

3 Conscientiousness;

4 Openness;

5 Neuroticism.

Each has an opposite and every individual's personality will be in a spectrum between the two. Of the above, it is neuroticism that causes the most difficulty because of its association with depression, anxiety and anger in most people's eyes. In some ways, 'sensitivity' would be a more neutral or utilitarian word. 'Sensitivity' can imply both a positive social gift *and* an emotionally negative reaction.

Behaviour and attitude

There are many other words that modify or amplify specific characteristics from the five personality characteristics above and these could include:

1 competitive, determined, demanding, assertive;

2 sociable, co-operative, empathetic, persuasive;

3 motivated, sincere, willing, committed;

4 open-minded, adventurous, curious, uninhibited;

5 sensitive, aware, concerned, involved.

Those above are on one end of the spectrum and the words below would be at the other end:

1 shy, retiring, nervous, modest;

2 cold, dismissive, suspicious, hostile;

3 indifferent, uninvolved, perfunctory, apathetic;

4 reactionary, biased, closed, dull;

5 insensitive, unaware, unconcerned, impassive.

The main issue is that personality and accompanying behaviours come in an unlimited array of guises. It is also the case that the meanings of the different words that can be used to describe someone are open to interpretation. They can, therefore, never be a fully accurate representation. As with the colours of the rainbow and in the context of understanding emotional intelligence, however, we are mainly concerned with primary characteristics that we can generally understand.

Another variant of the Five Factor Model above covers both ends of the spectrum and, for the sake of example, is shown in Table 2.1 below.

TABLE 2.1   Positioning matrix for your personal characteristics

Extrovert						Introvert
Accommodating						Resistant
Conscientious						Expedient
Open to experience						Closed to experience
Emotional						Stable

Emotional range

Emotions exist across a scale that covers the extremes and with many variations in between. They also manifest themselves in the type of personality you are both in your own and others' perception. From the Greeks onward, there are many theories and models to explain personality types but these usually boil down to just four or five main ones. The emotional range that someone has is usually between two points on a reactive–on-reactive scale. This will usually reinforce the perception of someone's personality type.

Many shades of pale

For example, in the range you might consider between *placid* and *angry* you could be *very placid*, *fairly placid*, *a little angry*, *quite angry* or *very angry indeed*. Whichever you were feeling would affect your behaviour and the impact of that behaviour on others.

In reality, the range will be more complex than that as it would be rare to feel *just placid* or *just angry*.

The impact of you being visibly and audibly placid will draw others towards you. Whereas if you are clearly and habitually angry, there will be more reticence to engage with you. Because the intercommunication is affected, so too may be the quality of the verbal transactions between you; likewise any choices and decisions that are made as a consequence. A wider emotional range gives you more opportunities to interact constructively (or destructively) with others whatever your personality type.

Learning and experience

What has been learned formally, and also learned from life and experience has an important bearing on someone's emotional capacity and behaviour.

People have different learning styles that correlate with Howard Gardner's 'multiple intelligence theory model'. These are to do with an individual's disposition towards linguistic, mathematical, visual, physical, musical, social and reflective mindsets. They show their likely abilities in words and language, use of logic, appreciation of image and space, use and control of the body, sound and rhythm, appreciation of others and capacity to think. Learning will be faster and more effective if achieved through their preferred orientation. These processes are also well understood as part of popular accelerated learning theory.

TABLE 2.2   The different ways people learn

Learning motivation	Possible areas of personal interest/capability
Linguistic	Reading, writing, verbal behaviours
Mathematical	Science, statistics, research, factual data
Visual	Diagrams, charts, pictures, photographs
Physical	Movement, sport, dance, physical form
Musical	Rhythm, sound, audible patterns, harmony
Social	People, behaviour, standards, groups
Reflective	Thinking, ideas, concepts, principles
Interpersonal	Friendship, rapport, co-operation, collective good

Learning attitudes and abilities

Anyone who has witnessed the products of a 'broken society' knows that those who did not have the chance, aptitude or motivation to learn will be disadvantaged generally. This is particularly apparent when they are called upon to make informed judgements that are based on their learning and experience.

The quality of learning and experience is a critical contributor to being able to apply learning and experience to emotions. Someone who has been inhibited by poverty, social attitudes or other disadvantages will not have been conditioned for good emotional judgement. Whereas those whose circumstances have not held them back in the same way will show much greater awareness and ability.

It may be that a trauma has affected motivation and resilience or it could be the 'brainwashing' of a peer group experience that has 'narrowed the arteries' so that situations are viewed in a restricted rather than open-minded way. The bottom line is that previous bad experiences will impair judgement unless steps have been taken to address the limitation.

Other experience

In arriving at an emotionally intelligent decision, the nature of previous experiences will influence judgement unless consciously factored out. Someone who has enjoyed success throughout most of their working life will more easily apply positive thinking to a decision than someone, say, whose work experiences have made him or her inclined to be cynical.

Goals, values, beliefs and prejudices

Your purpose in life may be to have a quiet, stress-free time or you may have something that drives you relentlessly in a particular direction. Driven people do not always 'arrive' at their goals. They are usually too busy seeking the next challenge rather than being content with reaching a specific destination in life. Whichever way you are, or whatever shade in between, the existence of goals influences the way you think, decide and act.

Who are you?

Your values, similarly, influence your response to any situation. They tend to be permanent rather than transitory aspects of your character. As such your values help determine 'who' you are. Beliefs are slightly different. They will have primarily been influenced by external experiences and learning but have since been 'hard-coded' into your emotional make-up. Finally, prejudices can be positive or negative. People tend to become resistant to anyone trying to change them and people even become proud of their prejudices.

Emotions

It is commonly understood that there are five primary emotions – love, happiness, anger, sadness and fear. Out of the basic five spring many more secondary emotions, or subtle shades of those emotions. Primary emotions are spontaneous responses to situations and almost impossible to resist. This is because they are part of the nervous system's hard-wired survival mechanisms. We may be able to modify the behaviour associated with those emotions.

It's in our nature

However, like all animals, we have to accept that they are a fundamental part of our nature. More subtle emotions have evolved with humans over time. This is frequently illustrated with a cross-section diagram of the human brain that shows the amygdala as the root of primary emotion (which we even share with dinosaurs) and evolved areas that include the frontal cortex, somatosensory cortex and hypothalamus.

FIGURE 2.4   Influences on emotionally intelligent decisions

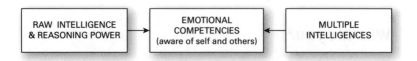

Raw intelligence and reasoning power

Commonly measured as IQ (Intelligence Quotient), intelligence has many different definitions. In simple terms it is the capacity that a person has to acquire knowledge, solve problems, engage in abstract as well as logical reasoning and articulate argument.

IQ is a single measure that compares a person's intelligence to a national average of 100. It derives from the work of Alfred Binet who, in 1905, devised tests to measure the intelligence of apparently backward children. The concept of IQ has thus endured for more than 100 years and is the definitive benchmark of cognitive intelligence.

It complements an individual's other emotional competencies.

Multiple intelligence

As defined by Howard Gardner, multiple intelligence includes not just cognitive ability but a wider set of aptitudes and predispositions. Because it also has a bearing on personality types and the types of emotion associated with those personalities, it has a strong bearing and influence on emotional intelligence.

His different types of intelligence are as shown below:

Intelligence type	Capability and perception
Linguistic	words and language
Logical–Mathematical	logic and numbers
Musical	music, sound, rhythm

Bodily–Kinaesthetic	body movement control
Spatial–Visual	images and space
Interpersonal	other people's feelings
Intrapersonal	self-awareness

As can be seen, particularly in the last two examples, there is a strong connection with emotional competencies.

Emotional competencies

Daniel Goleman identified five facets of emotional intelligence:

- knowing and understanding your own emotions;
- controlling your own emotions;
- understanding how to motivate yourself in particular ways;
- perceiving and understanding other people's emotions;
- knowing how to influence the emotions of others productively.

These are generally regarded as the main components of an emotional intelligence 'competency framework' but there are continuing debates around how you can measure the extent of each competency.

Cognitive intelligence, multiple intelligence and emotional competencies, then, contribute to the application of emotional intelligence as shown below.

Application of emotional intelligence

Emotional intelligence comprises the inputs from the previous three diagrams into this one (Figure 2.5). It is then used in making decisions that lead to actions that in turn lead to outcomes.

FIGURE 2.5   A process that produces the best results

It can be seen from the (often instantaneous) progression through conditioning factors, aptitudes and emotions shown in the previous diagrams that we reach a decision point. We then exercise what we should expect to be better judgement than if we had relied on emotions or intellect alone.

Measurement of EQ

Whereas IQ can be objectively measured, EQ has an emotional component for which there is no totally accurate means of measurement.

Self-assessment plays a part in measuring emotional intelligence but, however honest the responses are, must be seen as at least partially subjective in its results. Another way is to assess people's ability to reach decisions both with and without the emotional component, thus isolating it and being able to calculate the difference. Compared to IQ, EQ is a much more challenging measurement proposition and there are many methodologies, some popular and some serious. Both good and some bad methodologies are still proliferating.

Self-assessment is the most believable measurement tool

In the absence of more accurate forms of measurement, self-assessment is likely to be the most believable at this stage.

Emotional intelligence understanding continues to evolve thanks to bodies such as The Consortium for Research on Emotional Intelligence and a highly active worldwide community of psychologists and therapists. It is also gathering momentum because of businesses and other organizations seeking practical applications that will improve their strategy development, productivity and impact in certain areas. In particular the areas most affected are personnel selection, work performance, leadership and management.

Emotional intelligence has taken off in education

Increasingly, teachers are studying emotional intelligence with a view to understanding and dealing with the way that children in their care learn and behave. We know that the use and development of emotional intelligence provides ways of improving their chances in life and work.

Emotional intelligence is now a common factor in sales training. It is one of the areas where performance improvement is based on the use of both emotion and cognitive ability.

A characteristic of good leaders

Leadership development now relies on an understanding of emotional intelligence. In this case it relates to improving leadership effectiveness both in terms of the performance of people and in strategic and operational decision making.

A strong body of evidence now supports the view that the development of emotional intelligence in people and organizations has a dramatic and direct causal effect on performance.

Chapter 03
Ten character traits of emotionally intelligent people and ten of those who are not

Whether in a leadership, management or team role, those who achieve consistent success have a well-developed set of attributes that guide the way they work and live. By the same token, there are those whose emotionally intelligent attributes are notable by their absence and ten examples are given of both types.

Whether or not you already live up to these emotional intelligence attributes, they are ones that can be consciously learned and developed and in doing so can also 'infect' others. In the preservation of our species, our instincts are not just for personal survival. They are also for the common interest of the group. In looking after the group we also look after ourselves.

Social awareness is an essential part of emotional intelligence. This is particularly so in the workplace where the fundamental purpose is to combine our talents in a way that can produce bigger and better results than we are able to achieve on our own.

Those who practise and develop emotional intelligence both in themselves and in their organizations will improve productivity and multiply effectiveness. They will do this at a faster rate than those who are unaware of the benefits of emotional intelligence or, in some cases, think they know better.

The ten emotionally intelligent attributes are as follows.

1. Continuous striving for personal development

If people are always seeking improvement in some way or another, they cannot fail to grow. They have the energy and the interest, by definition, to seek longer-term success. They are often restless for skill, knowledge and new experiences. They are aware of where they are and where they want to be. But they are also aware of others and their feelings and ambitions. Others provide a benchmark that, as often as not, they want to equal or more probably exceed. They are naturally curious, observant and questioning.

2. Unrelenting commitment to support others' interests

Emotional intelligence espouses social awareness and belief in the symbiotic outcome of co-operating with others. If others are supporting you, as compared to opposing you, they will seek opportunities to reciprocate. The social model exists for the greater good of the group. So, by opting out of it you reduce the chances of leveraged achievement. If your support for others' interests is just posturing in order to create a personal advantage, in the long run you will fail.

3. Clarity of intentions

If you don't know where you want to get to, you will have no control over your future. Any route will do and you could end up nowhere in particular, or even back or behind where you started. Such is the power and adaptability of the human mind that if you have a clear purpose you will find the resources to achieve what you want. But this is provided you put in the necessary drive and determination to get there. Intentions are projections into the future and so lead to more emotionally intelligent judgements and decisions.

4. Sustaining positive values

As mentioned previously, positive thought creates positive actions that lead to positive results. Values are a permanent part of your make-up and were formed early in your life. Your values mean that you always have guiding principles for your attitudes and behaviour. This influences the decisions you take and that will invariably be aimed at creating something good. Focusing on the positive will shape others' attitudes too and increases the chance of their greater benefit.

5. Listening and observation

If we are inwardly focused and concerned more about ourselves than others, we do not gather the information and knowledge that equips us to interact productively. Emotionally intelligent people think beyond their 'bubble' and consider the wider ramifications of choices and decisions. They include others in their thinking and factor their likely emotional responses into the equation. Essentially, they are gaining feedback that leads to the likelihood of a better outcome.

6. Objectivity

Try as we might to suppress them, we all have our prejudices. Emotionally intelligent people will have a better-developed facility to suspend judgement in favour of waiting until more facts are known. A prejudice is a skewed emotion. Emotional intelligence is about the balance of emotion and intellect and so requires objectivity if it is to lead to the best available outcome. It can sometimes be irritating to others if someone always insists on being 'fair'. This negates the opportunity for a strongly felt opinion. How you handle this objectivity requires emotional intelligence because the strongly felt opinion is a valid contributor to a balanced argument – provided there is scope to include an alternative view. If you know the extremes you have a better chance of making a balanced decision.

7. Challenging the status quo

'Reasonable people adapt themselves to the world. Unreasonable people attempt to adapt the world to themselves. All progress, therefore, depends on unreasonable people', said George Bernard Shaw. Unreasonable people will not be content with the status quo and have a driving compulsion to challenge and to create change. This is entirely compatible with an emotionally intelligent approach that seeks a preferred outcome rather than the automatic acceptance of the validity of an initial response. The word 'unreasonable' itself indicates a preference for emotion over reason. However, that emotion often ends up being more productive because it combines the two. Solutions where everyone ends up happy almost always involve some kind of contradiction or compromise.

8. Taking the longer view

The French word for far-sighted is 'presbyte'. Although lost in the mists of time, it is the root for 'Presbyterian', a church denomination whose elders (or presbyters) were chosen and ordained for their long-sighted wisdom. In many cultures, great age equates with wisdom, but in other cultures it equates to resistance to change and progress. Long-sightedness is the prerogative of both young and old. It is a question of using learning and experience to convert emotion and intellect, through emotional competence, into rational thought. Those who take the longer view are already practising emotional intelligence.

9. Converting negative inclinations into positive thought

Everyone, however positive he or she would normally be, at some time or other feels low, dejected, devoid of energy and lacking in confidence. Those who practise better emotional intelligence are able to derive positive value from negative emotions and have developed techniques to do so. This is a definite area of life where emotional intelligence can be developed in those whose natural inclinations are negative.

10. Nurturing the team

A characteristic of emotionally intelligent people is that they recognize that although individuals may not be perfect, a team could be. They strive to ensure that different types of contribution to an endeavour are recognized and promoted. They know that it is the outcome of collective effort that produces the optimum result – not just the star qualities of specific players. A good analogy is Rugby Union football where it takes a combination of different types of body, athleticism, capabilities and roles to produce a smooth and unified performance.

　　Each of the above characteristics breaks down into a further list of emotional competencies that includes those conventionally listed in emotional intelligence literature and referred to in the chapter on 'Building Blocks'.

The ten characteristics of less emotionally intelligent people are as follows.

1. Assume that something good will turn up

People do not always connect what needs to happen with making it happen. They are good about making observations on what *should* happen but more reluctant to take on the responsibility for doing something about it. As other people are often more proactive than they are, and can be relied on to get things done, they are inclined to believe, rightly in many cases, that something *will* turn up.

2. See things only through their own eyes

In the same way that horses were given blinkers to keep them focused only on the road ahead, some people are equally limited in their lack of an open-minded acceptance of others' views. These limitations can be because of personality or because it suits them best if they do not have to debate with others. In some cases, although appearing strong, they may, in reality, be insecure.

3. Are imprecise about their goals

If you don't know what your goals are you cannot be blamed for not achieving them. Life is full of choices. This, rightly or wrongly, gives people the opportunity to equivocate and this means that it is harder to commit to a specific direction. It may also be that they cannot clearly visualize what success might look like and this therefore limits their ambition.

4. Follow the crowd before they follow their conscience

Group behaviour is a powerful opiate that can dull people's senses as to what is right. This is why normally well-intentioned people will do unacceptable things in specific circumstances and is, of course, what fuels riots, revolutions and anti-social behaviour. They follow the crowd to make the 'right impression' not because they have thought through the consequences of their actions. In a work or business context, this is going with the flow rather than striving to make a positive personal impact.

5. Reject the opinions of those they perceive to lack authority

Some people judge the person rather than the opinion. If they think the owner of a particular opinion is of a lower status than they are, they find it easy to dismiss both the person and the opinion. They may accept the opinion of a superior as he or she 'knows best' even though they may have rejected that opinion from someone else.

6. Don't want to believe they can change themselves or others

It is sometimes easier to accept the status quo than face the battle to change things. So, for example, the belief that 'I will never be any good at selling' is a self-fulfilling prophecy that denies the fact that humans are exceptionally adaptable given the will and determination to be so. In this particular instance, by changing themselves, they will automatically be able to influence change in others.

7. Put status before authority

However important you are, when taken to hospital, you will defer to clinicians that know best. If you were to insist on a particular procedure against their wishes you would be applying the wrong values and attempting to negate their authority. Telling people to do something 'because I'm your manager' is less effective in the long run than being a good leader who people will naturally follow.

8. React on impulse not thought

Human beings can use their minds to decide how they will react to particular situations. If they are angry then that is their choice and not an inevitability. Emotional intelligence is about displacing a spontaneous emotion with one that will lead to a better outcome. Fight or flight is a basic animal instinct that we human beings have learned to control in the interests of our species... but sometimes ignore.

9. Are pessimistic in the face of change

Optimists, it has been shown, are likely to be consistently more successful than pessimists. The issue is, however, that change is disruptive and often regarded as negative by those who perceive themselves as 'victims' of that disruption. Sometimes it may be the fault of those initiating the change not communicating the benefits that will outweigh the disruption, but as often as not it is the pessimistic attitude that prevails.

10. Communicate what they think people want to hear

It is a sign of strength to be able to give bad news, but lack of confidence in people as to how they will be perceived often leads to expediency rather than candour. The best leaders are able to impart bad news as well as good. They know that it enhances their credibility to do so and engenders trust. 'Little white lies' may be acceptable in trivial circumstances but people mostly do not want to be robbed of the truth and will detect when they are being told what others think they want to hear.

Chapter 04
Emotions and their impact on work and life

Whether it's getting on with others, reacting to situations at home or at work or simply reflecting on life's purpose, our emotions play a critical part in defining who we are, what we want to achieve and our effectiveness in managing our routes to success. In the 11 sections that follow are the opportunities and challenges we face and the considerations we need to take into account in positioning ourselves as, or to become, emotionally intelligent people. Essentially, the sections are about life skills but it is the application of those life skills that will make a difference.

1. Self-awareness – recognizing your own emotional make-up

The sign of intelligent people is their ability to control emotions by the application of reason. **MAYA MANNES**

Self-awareness is a requisite of personal competence. Self-awareness can be split into three parts: emotional self-awareness, accurate self-assessment and self-confidence. Emotional self-awareness is acknowledging what you feel about situations and how they affect you. Accurate self-assessment requires an examination of your own strengths and weaknesses. Self-confidence is being sure of your own self-worth and what you are capable of achieving. In order to be able to manage yourself, your emotions and your actions you need to *know* yourself.

Self-awareness and self-consciousness

Self-awareness is related to, but not identical with, self-consciousness. John Locke spent almost 20 years of his life studying the subject of 'self-awareness'. In his *An Essay Concerning Human Understanding* (1689) Locke suggests that personal identity (the self) 'depends on consciousness, not on substance'. Following his argument, we are the same person to the extent that we are conscious of our past and future thoughts and actions in the same way that we are conscious of our present thoughts and actions. Self-awareness theory states that when we focus on ourselves, we evaluate and compare our current behaviour to our internal standards and values. Various emotional states are intensified by self-awareness. People can be negatively affected if they don't live up to their personal standards. In simple terms, aids to self-awareness include mirrors, an audience, being videotaped or recorded. These cues also increase accuracy of personal memory.

Remember: As you grow in self-awareness you understand more about why you feel whatever you feel and why you behave as you behave.

When considering emotional intelligence and how it can help you in your career, self-awareness is an important aspect of it. Unless you know who you are, self-acceptance and change become impossible. How can you possibly make decisions and choices in life, and in the workplace, if you don't understand why you want what you do want? It would be chaotic, if not impossible, to exist purely for the moment, never knowing what you were going to do next. If you were looking for good, sound information on a particular subject you'd probably turn to an expert. So who is the best person to ask for information about yourself? You. Why? Because you live inside your head and your body day in, day out.

How self-aware are you?

Questioning helps everyone become more self-aware; the more meaningful the question, the closer people get to who they really are. As you begin your personal 'Spanish Inquisition' bear in mind that unspecific answers will only give you a general idea of who you are. The important thing is to be precise; the more specific you can be, the clearer the picture you will get. Being completely honest when you answer leads to greater self-awareness, but that does require courage. The answers should reveal whether these are thoughts or actual feelings that you experience in certain situations.

For example, if you want to find out about social aspects of your life, you should ask yourself what types of people you enjoy spending time with. How would you describe them? Are they intelligent, open-minded, lively, reflective, amusing, optimistic, pessimistic, sporty or perceptive? Make a list of qualities drawn from the people you like, then ask yourself why you enjoy those specific qualities. Is it because these people are similar to yourself, or different from you? Do you have many friends of the kind you've described? Where did you meet these people? Was it through work, family, community, childhood or online?

On an emotional level, you could question yourself about in which three recent situations you were happiest. Cite specific instances, and list what elements were present at the time. What were you feeling at those times? Ask yourself about your worst fears right now. When do you feel most angry or upset? What is it about those situations that makes you feel that way? Do you have control over your emotions? Depending on the answer, ask yourself why, or why not.

You can go on and on, for example, reflecting on significant relationships in your life; spiritual and ethical issues; financial, career, values and personal matters. Finally, to help you become fully self-aware, you should investigate your personal definitions of some common words. Not until you come up with your own definitions will the meaning become clear. Here are a few to consider:

- happiness;
- success;

- trust;
- acceptance;
- anger;
- responsibility;
- love;
- guilt;
- judgement;
- reality.

Remember: Self-awareness should be the route to understanding, which should lead to the ability to make informed choices about how to behave in situations.

What we pursue in life (relationships, financial independence, charity work/volunteering) increases and enhances our physical and emotional development. Self-awareness is a function of perception and observation and as such is closely allied to emotional intelligence. Remember that some animals have proved they have a degree of self-awareness – dolphins, gorillas and elephants recognize themselves in a mirror, which indicates intelligence. But humans are more than self-aware; we are aware that we are aware (for example, you might remark to a friend 'isn't this a strange conversation we're having?'). 'Who am I?' is a fundamental question and there is no definitive answer. People's observation of their own behaviour should provide clues as to who they are, but it will only be part of the explanation.

Exercise

Try the following exercise to see who you are and what influences you. The questions are based loosely on the Belbin team roles (the work of Meredith Belbin and researchers at Henley Management College UK) defined some years ago. Something similar is often used in psychometric testing.

Tick the answer that best describes your response or behaviour:

1 I like to

work hard and enjoy finishing a job
ignore deadlines
work with people rather than alone
do what I want to get the job done regardless of others

2 I sometimes get upset when other people slow up my work

yes
no

3 I do my best work as part of a team/working with others by

showing great patience
pushing others to their limit
letting others set the priorities
setting work goals together

4 I like to help others with their work

yes
no

5 When people come to see me at work

I like to chat with them
I let them sort out their own problems
I spend a lot of time listening to them
I become impatient

6 I constantly check to see how others are getting on with their work

yes
no

7 When someone delegates a task to me, I prefer to

be given total responsibility
set early deadlines
plan to do the work with others
be patient

8 I prefer others to be in charge

yes

no

9 I avoid wasting time by

getting through things quickly
showing concern for others
leaving others alone
rewarding others for their help/teamwork

10 I am always early for meetings

yes

no

11 I encourage my friends/co-workers by

being friendly towards them
setting hard-and-fast deadlines
working as a team
avoiding conflict

12 Friendship is more important than work

yes

no

13 When my work schedule gets behind due to others, I feel

very stressed
concern for others
that it is someone else's fault
that the problem needs solving together

14 I plan my tasks way ahead of the deadline to avoid failing

yes

no

15 I get added value in my work by

developing a network with other people
encouraging a relaxed atmosphere
using a team approach
stretching my team/co-workers

16 I always say 'thank you' if someone has helped me

yes

no

NB There is no point scoring here because it is not so important in this context. The purpose is to see whether you are aware of others when you work, whether they motivate or irritate you and how much this affects the way you behave. Do you prefer to work uninterrupted or does the behaviour, mood and the action of your colleagues affect the way you conduct yourself at work? However, a qualitative analysis of the above will help define your underlying nature.

2. The different effects of positive and negative emotions

Taken in simple form, one way to define the effects of positive emotions is that they create an upward spiral. Negative emotions, on the other hand, can contribute to the creation of a downward progression. Everyone, from an early age to the latter stages of life, is encouraged to be positive. People are urged to 'look on the bright side of life' (with appropriate amount of credit being given to the Monty Python Team in the film, *Life of Brian*). It is considered healthier to have positive thoughts and emotions than negative ones.

So why should we think positively? What effect does it have on us? We know that an optimist is someone who looks at a glass of wine and sees it being half full rather than half empty. But do we know how it's done? How can people make themselves feel positive? There is no switch on the side of your head that you can press; standing on one leg and whistling a tune from *The Sound of Music* may work for some people, but is not necessarily a universally approved method of being happy.

The purpose of emotions

Remember: Emotions have a purpose. If positive emotions help us to thrive, negative emotions can also help us survive.

Negative emotions can act as a protection against life-threatening situations so (paradoxically) they do have a positive effect in some cases. Anger and fear trigger the fight or flight reflexes, so when we feel these emotions we either attack what we're afraid of or run away. Disgust makes us wary of toxic or harmful substances. It is when negative emotions are overused that they aren't so helpful. They can make us ill and unable to function normally. Fearful people become phobic, feel threatened by people or events: in some extreme cases they are unable to leave their homes, do not trust strangers, and are unable to cope with things that positive people would normally take in their stride.

When you think of positive emotions (happiness, optimism, love, pleasure, gratitude, delight, ecstasy) you feel energized. You are more likely to take positive steps to improve the quality of your life, relationships or emotional well-being. It is most people's wish to be positive all the time because it can be life-enhancing. Avoidance of threatening situations increases the likelihood of being happy. A positive outlook on life has a broad spectrum, whereas a negative one narrows thinking and actions.

Positive emotions

Positive people are proactive. They are more likely to take action than people who are negative or depressed. They do not fear the unknown and are prepared to 'give something a go' whether or not they will achieve success. Some people find they are more positive when the weather is good. Sunlight has a beneficial effect on a lot of us and this makes it easier to get out of bed in the morning.

When it is dark, cold and damp it takes a lot more effort to do something – even something as mundane as going to work or taking the dog out.

People who are habitually positive – and some people are natural optimists – are more likely to be extrovert characters. They have an aptitude for coping with a wide range of activities and personalities. They also have a more highly developed sense of emotional well-being. They tend to develop long-term plans and goals. There is some proof that patients who maintain a positive attitude can overcome illness more quickly and cope better with adversity than more negative characters.

Certain positive attitudes are what help employees cope with stress-related issues at work. Even in bereavement, people with a positive approach adapt quicker to their loss and set new personal goals and objectives.

Negative emotions

People who tend toward negative emotions, on the other hand, are not expansive in their outlook. They can be severely introverted and have little awareness of other people and their emotions and attitudes. Negative types don't believe there's much point in planning for next year, they are too busy worrying about the meteor strike that they've just read in the paper is expected to annihilate our planet sometime later in the year. They see no point in booking their next year's holiday if the whole of the universe is to be pulverized before winter arrives.

Negativity dampens any enthusiasm. People who are depressed, anxious or irritated are difficult to spend time with. So there is a self-fulfilling prophecy here; negative people think others don't like them, they are awkward in social situations, people leave them alone. They then have incontrovertible proof that no one likes them and whatever they do things never improve. They reach a point when they feel that life has no meaning. They feel that they are failures and life has let them down. It is rarely their fault, they have an uncanny ability to apportion blame in any direction other than their own.

The effect of emotions

The problem with negative emotions is that people miss cues and opportunities that the more optimistic person embraces with enthusiasm. It is not difficult to see who, say, at a business-networking event is likely to gain something positive from the experience. A negative person would start from the point of view of networking being a waste of time. How can they possibly meet anyone of interest in a room full of strangers? Everyone is bound to be dull, so they don't show any interest in any person present. The net result? They stand alone like a wallflower for a while and then quit the room. This proves to their own satisfaction that they were right: networking was just a waste of their time.

On the other hand the optimistic person, who has a positive approach to meeting new people, makes an effort to talk to some of those they're meeting for the first time. They show an appropriate amount of curiosity and ask questions that are not threatening. Within a few minutes some connection is formed – they have a mutual friend, they attended the same university, their families both originate from a particular part of the country – it starts an exchange that could lead to a friendship under the right circumstances. Without a positive emotional attitude this sort of coincidence *never* happens. But the reverse is *always* true.

In extreme cases, pessimism and hopelessness discourage people from taking action at the right time or the right place. The feedback from worsening circumstances, such as breakdowns in relationships, redundancy, health problems, creates an ever-increasing sense of failure for an individual. They reach a point where they are convinced that nothing will ever go right and this becomes their reality.

As mentioned earlier, positive emotions provide a trend towards uplifting attitudes, hopes and aspirations. They can help people recognize a beneficial opportunity, take advantage of an encouraging event, which generates more chances to broaden horizons and embrace new experiences.

This open-minded approach is healthy, holistic and emotionally intelligent.

3. Self-confidence and how it can be developed

Self-confidence is the first requisite to great undertakings.

SAMUEL JOHNSON (1709-84)

Emotionally intelligent people come across as stable, grounded people with an awareness of situations pertaining to themselves and beyond their own personal perspective. They exhibit an attitude of self-confidence. As described above, those who have accurately assessed what sort of people they are, how situations, circumstances and people affect them are likely to be more confident and assured. People who are self-confident believe they can do anything they choose and be competent at any activity they decide to pursue. Sometimes a person can be fully confident in one area but completely lacking in another. Take for example a sports person showing amazing abilities in his own field of expertise but freezing in front of an audience when having to make an acceptance speech at an awards ceremony. Self-confidence can vary from place to place and hour to hour. You may be feeling perfectly happy and confident; suddenly something upsets you, doubts come flooding in to your mind and you feel shaken and unsure.

Confidence

Confidence comprises a number of self-images: physical; emotional; intellectual and social. You also have a 'real' self-image and an 'ideal' one: that is to say the way you *really* are and how you would *like* to be. Most people have definite opinions about their appearance (usually these centre around how it could be improved). Physical self-image is important because while you can try to improve it, ultimately what matters is that you are happy with yourself as you are.

Remember: Emotions are an important factor governing self-confidence. A positive, enthusiastic and happy person feels good; whereas in contrast, someone who is a worrier or feels guilty or angry about things often has a poor opinion of themselves.

Emotional self-image

Your emotional self-image can be improved by choosing positive emotions. Remember you can always choose your own thoughts. Intellect is something that you were either born with, or was formed during the early part of your school days. Most people are cleverer than they think they are. Those who hold self-limiting beliefs could, if they wished, probably trace these back to childhood. The most important factor in determining whether someone develops intellectual ability is the expectation of others, initially parents and teachers. Your social self-image is what *you* think other people think of you. Don't confuse this with what others actually do think of you. There are many people who go through agonies thinking that others have a poor opinion of them when it is not the case at all. It is always nice to be thought well of by friends and colleagues, but don't be ruled by what you imagine other people think. The important thing is what opinion you have of yourself.

Your 'real' self-image is how you view yourself right now. Your feelings of worth and fulfilment are directly related to it. Your 'ideal' self-image is how you would like to be. Can you imagine what your life would be like if you had all the qualities you've always dreamed of? It is difficult for anyone to rise above their level of self-esteem, which is why building self-confidence is so important. Confidence to a large extent allows you to live the life you want.

How self-esteem helps

People with high self-esteem don't allow others' attitudes or behaviour to influence their beliefs about themselves. They rely on what they expect of themselves; which is all that matters. Setting your own standards helps you avoid judging yourself by other people's standards. It is easy to be fooled by society's view that appearance, intelligence and material wealth are the main criteria for assessing someone's worth. These are actually superficial attributes and they are not as important as people think. One of the most effective ways of growing in confidence is to learn how to handle criticism. This requires an ability to think on your feet, and not to take the criticism personally.

If someone rudely points out that your garden is full of weeds and rubbish and you ought to deal with it, don't automatically apologize. You might explain that once the builders have finished fitting your new kitchen, you will be sorting out the garden. In the meantime it would be pointless to do so while they are still working and using it as a dumping ground.

Train yourself to become immune to whatever someone throws at you. After all, you can't expect other people to treat you the way you would like all the time. Most important of all, stand up for yourself and behave in an assertive way whenever possible. However difficult this seems at first, it does get easier the more you do it.

Confidence test

To assess how confident you are, you should aim for a 'yes' answer to all of the following questions. For those answering honestly, don't be disheartened if 'no' and 'sometimes' are what you've replied. Should you score five 'yes's you can skip to the next section.

1 Do you like yourself?

2 Do you avoid criticizing yourself?

3 Are you confident about your intellectual abilities?

4 When you look in the mirror, do you respect the person you see?

5 Is the person you see someone you really want to be?

If you can develop a feeling of confidence in yourself, others will become aware of it and start treating you with more respect. This in turn creates more confidence within you. A positive self-image creates the belief that others see you more positively and have higher expectations of you. This leads you to perform better, and your good performance confirms your better feelings about yourself. This feedback reinforces your improving self-image, and so on and so on.

Persuasive thinking

Remember: When trying to improve your self-confidence, never underestimate the power of the mind. Thoughts have tremendous power – they can build you up or bring you down. It all depends on which ones you allow to prevail.

Positive thoughts are harder to hold on to. The negative ones (maddeningly) can stick around for days on end. Being aware of the power of thought, and the inevitability of cause and effect, will set you on the path to success. To get the right results, think the right thoughts.

The brain has two parts (sometimes called hemispheres), each of which has its own special function. The left brain (the conditioned mind) deals with analysing, logic and evaluating. It tackles processes but can only process one piece of information at a time. The right brain (the reflective mind) is the creative side. It senses rather than thinks and can handle lots of information at any one time. It knows what's right and wrong, and sees the links between cause and effect without judging, criticizing or condemning.

The mind has a neat way of convincing itself that it is right. If an idea seems reasonable and the mind accepts it as true, it tends to become reality. If on the other hand you think you can't do something, then you expect to fail and you most likely will. If you allow yourself to think you are useless, the other side of your brain will seek the proof it needs so that you are not disappointed. However, when you think you can do something and believe it, then you will set about proving it. How many times have you seen sportsmen or teams competing in a desperate power struggle? Attitude of mind is key – the power of positive thought often is the deciding factor in who wins and who loses.

In simple terms self-confidence is just a collection of thoughts about yourself. Since you can control your thoughts, you can choose to be confident, or not. Every 'cause' has an 'effect'. Thoughts are causes, actions are effects. Positive thinking inevitably leads to positive actions. Your mind has a conscious element and an unconscious one. Your unconscious mind doesn't know the difference between thoughts, imagination and external events. The thoughts you choose filter into your unconscious mind where they control your future. It is crucial to success to become aware the instant you are thinking negatively and stop. Banish the harmful thought and replace it with a helpful, confident one.

4. Motivation, persistence and belief

Ability is what you're capable of doing. Motivation determines what you do. Attitude determines how well you do it.

LOU HOLTZ

An important aspect of personal competence is having the combined attributes of motivation, persistence and belief. Motivation can be defined as an internal condition that triggers behaviour and gives it direction. It energizes and directs goal-oriented behaviour. Motivation can be split into two parts: intrinsic and extrinsic. The former derives from rewards inherent to a specific task or activity: the enjoyment of reading an exciting book or finally solving a difficult puzzle. The latter comes from outside the activator – such as a monetary reward or fear of punishment. Persistence is associated with self-discipline. It is in essence the ability to maintain action regardless of your emotions. For example, consider an explorer trying to reach the South Pole. He may be on the point of collapse from exhaustion, with painful frostbitten feet, but he keeps on walking through blizzards and freezing temperatures because he knows that if he doesn't reach safety and shelter he will certainly perish. Motivation and persistence are interlinked.

Remember: When you are engaged on a difficult task your motivation levels may rise and fall depending on your mood. Motivation alone is not sufficient to produce results, but persistence harnessed to motivation will.

Imagine the situation if someone is desperate to give up smoking. Everyone knows that the hardest part is the first few days. It is difficult to stop yourself reaching for the packet of cigarettes whenever you have a spare moment because that is an habitual action. In the beginning you are highly motivated, you resist temptation, knowing that if you persist you will be healthier as a result. Persistence will get you through those first crucial days. Once you realize you can survive without lapsing, your motivation to keep off the cigarettes will increase.

Belief is part of the process, in that it is the knowledge aspect. Continuing with the giving up smoking analogy, everyone knows that smoking is not good for their health. Therefore your belief is that once you've given up smoking you will be healthier and live longer. The concept of belief presumes that there is a subject (the believer) and an object of belief (the proposition). Beliefs are sometimes divided into *core beliefs* (the ones you may be actively thinking about) and *dispositional beliefs* (those you may feel confident about but have never previously given thought to). The latter are a bit odd because they are views that you hold without having spent much time thinking about them. For example, if someone asked you if you believed that penguins wear raincoats, you might answer emphatically that they do not. But you haven't any proof nor have you thought about the possibility before being asked such a question.

5. Getting on with others

Small communities grow great through harmony, great ones fall to pieces through discord.   **SALLUST (86 BC–34 BC)**

The ability to get along with other people, particularly in the workplace, is important. One of the reasons for this is that most professionals spend at least a third of their life at work. Emotionally intelligent people are *unconsciously* conscious of how people interact with each other. They don't make mistakes when communicating with others – whichever means are being employed. The ability to get on with other people is a core competency that everyone has. But some people possess it to a far greater degree than others. Some people possess the skill but rarely use it, and then wonder why they often find life more difficult than other people.

Remember: People skills are essential if you wish to be successful in your dealings with others. This in turn affects your quality of life. The better skilled you are at communicating, the more likely you are to have reasonable relationships with people.

Everyone benefits if there is a relaxed, friendly atmosphere in which to exist; frosty, tense, hostile environments aren't conducive to people thriving or enjoying themselves. This applies in both social and workplace situations.

Basic rules

There are some basic rules that most people already know which prevent others being 'rubbed up the wrong way'. Unfortunately, at times, say, when under pressure or concentrating deeply about an important matter, these things get forgotten. It is very easy under these circumstances to find that other people respond negatively towards you.

Observing boundaries (social and spatial) is one key habit. People have certain customs that are important to them and definite ideas as to their personal space. This can include enquiries about their family life, property, finances, politics or religion. Respect for others is an important part of getting along well in relationships. You will soon realize if you have overstepped the mark when an otherwise pleasant exchange turns nasty – quickly. It is best to apologize and remember the sensitive areas when communicating in future. Someone's personal space is sacrosanct and it is upsetting to have it encroached upon – whether this is by verbal means or physical. Be aware and responsive to other people's feelings.

Keeping promises is another 'make or break' habit. At work or in private life, no one likes being let down by other people. When you make a commitment to someone, you must honour it. If you know you will have difficulty in keeping your promise, don't make it in the first place. Trustworthiness is the currency of most relationships.

If someone asks you to respect a confidence and you fail, there is no easier way of ruining a friendship. Follow through on your personal and professional commitments to everyone. If your reputation is ever questioned, your friends and colleagues are more likely to reserve judgement, or give you the benefit of the doubt, if they respect you and have no reason to think you would let them down.

Having respect for other people's time is another aspect of people skills. This involves being aware when someone is in a hurry, or what their natural rhythm is. The ability to tune in to other people's 'clock' helps to keep relationships smooth particularly in the workplace. Everyone knows that some colleagues are not good in the morning. Their desire is to be spared the normal pleasantries until at least their second cup of coffee. Yet others find it very important to be spoken to, even if it is just a simple 'Hello' or 'Good morning', when you see them. They would feel slighted if they were ignored, however busy you or they are. Being conscious of other people's time restraints is a sign of courtesy and emotional intelligence. Don't expect a gossip each time you pass someone's desk. Pick up on people's individual tempos. If someone is glancing at their watch, don't detain them in lively banter in the corridor. This is insensitive and extremely irritating.

Curiosity about other people is an essential part of getting along with them. If you are not interested in other people, they will not be particularly interested in you. Asking questions doesn't mean finding out every minute detail about their life history. But it would be far easier to ask first if someone is a vegetarian, before inviting them to a barbecue where all they will get to eat is a lettuce leaf. Colleagues prefer to be consulted on matters – which form of communication is preferable for example: phone, e-mail, letter or personal visit? Show respect for them by responding appropriately. If in doubt, ask – politely – and you will find that your ability to get on with others is enhanced. Showing concern for others' feelings is a good way to begin friendships.

Listening. When someone speaks to you, you should pay attention. The ability to listen to colleagues, friends, family, strangers shows that you have emotional intelligence. You will then be able to deal with them in an appropriate way. Most people talk far more than they listen. Getting along with other people well requires highly developed listening skills. It is also important to pay attention not only to what is said, but also what remains unsaid. This is part of social awareness – picking up on other communication methods besides verbal ones. These include body language, vocal tone and physical gestures. If you think you may be weak in this area, it is well worth getting some training. Possessing these skills makes establishing good relationships with other people a whole lot easier. By developing your listening and understanding, colleagues and other people will know that their thoughts and feelings are being appreciated and accepted.

Checking emotions. Emotional check-ups are another good interpersonal skill to develop. Pay attention to what your instincts are telling you; about your work, your relationships with colleagues, or anything that makes you think something may be amiss. If you think something is wrong, find out. Should a colleague behave in an unusual way (he is late arriving at work, seems distant and unable to concentrate) enquire if there's anything wrong. He may tell you, in which case perhaps you can help him sort out the problem so that things can get back on track. Addressing miscues and miscommunications at home or in the workplace prevents relationships from getting out of shape or breaking down. No problem gets better by being ignored. An emotional health-check is a great way of spotting signs of trouble before they escalate.

The ability to get on with others is essential. It means that you are able to communicate (transmit and receive signals) effectively. It helps to improve personal productivity at work and attain a high level of quality relationships both inside and outside your job. You show a healthy awareness of what is going on around you both physically and psychologically. Keeping your interpersonal skills highly tuned requires effort and time – but it is well worth it.

6. The value and challenges of social awareness

Educate your children to self-control, to the habit of holding passion and prejudices and evil tendencies subject to an upright and reasoning will, and you have done much to abolish misery from their future and crimes from society.

BENJAMIN FRANKLIN (1706–90)

Social awareness is sometimes described as 'social and emotional learning'. An individual who has the ability to recognize and manage his emotions, develop care and concern for others, make responsible decisions, establish positive relationships and handle challenging situations effectively is someone who has the attributes of social awareness. In brief, socially aware people can manage themselves, relate well with others and make good decisions. Certain jobs require people to possess higher levels of social awareness (such as priest, social worker, charity volunteer) than others.

Remember: Social awareness involves being able to see things in perspective, showing empathy with others, appreciating that not everyone is the same and respecting their differences.

The value of social awareness is that it impacts on a person's character and their citizenship. Character is shown through the way we live; how many social and emotional competencies we demonstrate. To be an effective person at work you should be able to demonstrate self-management, problem-solving ability, decision-making aptitude, clear communication skills and be proficient at managing workplace relationships. Translated into the wider community, if you demonstrate these qualities when interacting in your local neighbourhood, city or at a national level, these are the core competencies of social awareness.

The benefits of social and emotional skills

Social and emotional skills help people become good citizens. This includes making contributions to civic life and humanitarian work (such as volunteering to help socially challenged minority groups). Good citizens are those who behave well personally and socially. They are responsible, they look after their health by exercising restraint with regard to diet and exercise. They exercise self-control so that they don't get stressed or overreact in challenging situations. In schools and universities, conscientious students are those who are most likely to have sound social and emotional skills. Whether these have been learned in the classroom and reinforced in the home environment is not clear. However, it takes a degree or two of self-control to concentrate on finishing off an essay that needs to be handed in on time when your friends are at the door urging you to leave it to go out drinking with them or attend a party. People who are able to control their emotions (such as anger or anxiety) are more likely to contribute to society in a healthy way. Good citizens could also be described as effective workers: they possess skills that make them employable and productive.

The challenges of social awareness

The challenges of social awareness are where people have not been taught these skills in schools or have not been given good role models during their upbringing. Someone who has been raised without social awareness is going to find it hard to control their emotions and behaviour. Schools have a responsibility to teach social awareness and values in the formal and informal curriculum. But it is a real challenge to equip a young person with such core competencies if there is no reinforcement of the same values within the family unit. Teachers are important role models of the competencies of self- and social-awareness, self-management, relationship management and responsible decision making. It is an uphill task when outside of the learning environment these skills are not upheld. Children who do not possess sound social and emotional skills and anchored values will find it difficult to demonstrate good character or citizenship.

They may have low self-esteem and be challenged when it comes to contributing effectively in any employment they attain.

Remember: When people are blind to the effects of how their own actions impact on others, it is vital to help them realize how others are viewing them.

In order to encourage the development of core social competencies it is important to impress on people the 'cultural requirement' of, say, the classroom, lecture hall or workplace. For example, if someone persistently swears at work, it will be necessary for someone in authority to say that 'we don't allow that here'. If that fails, a stricter 'stop it' followed by a punitive measure may be necessary. The purpose of this is to help the person realize that there are consequences to his actions. If a particular form of behaviour is not condoned because it is inconsiderate, embarrassing or hurtful, it is essential that the perpetrator of the action becomes aware of this.

One of the major challenges for people who lack social awareness is that it prevents them from achieving their full potential and in a worst-case scenario they become socially excluded. How can they become high achievers (or even moderate achievers) if they are so occupied in trying to manage their own behaviour that they are unable to take advantage of education or job-skills training? Should young people carry the burden of social adversity (poverty, experience of violence, lack of adequate health care) they are at high risk of developing social problems. In other words they are ill-equipped to deal with the social issues that surround them. The need to recognize these problems is overwhelming and essential. The challenges presented by members of society who do not possess social awareness are everywhere; the strategies for dealing with them however in many cases are not.

7. Men v women

It isn't just a matter of applying emotional intelligence, the fact is that men and women both think and communicate differently.

These differences cause misunderstandings, which in turn provoke more crossed wires. They can make everyone feel angry or upset; particularly in the workplace where people can experience being undervalued or excluded. This leads to companies failing to hold on to excellent employees because when someone feels powerless to do anything to change a situation for the better, the natural reaction is to escape.

Gender-related behaviour can create situations where talented workers feel excluded but they don't know why. This happens because men and women see situations differently, hear things in other ways, assimilate facts by alternative means and communicate dissimilarly. The challenges created by gender differences can be overcome to a large extent by learning how to make the most of your own strengths as well as those of the other sex.

How to pick up on gender-related behaviour

There are ways to overcome misunderstandings caused by gender differences. By putting yourself in the other person's shoes, listening carefully and avoiding common communication errors, it is possible to get your message across clearly without causing offence. It is also a part of emotional intelligence that you seek to understand the situation from their point of view.

One of the workplace issues caused by gender difference that can be helped by applying EQ is a high staff turnover – directors or managers need to work out why so many people leave and what causes the situation. Unhappy employees leave – happy employees stay – so you need to apply EQ to keep employees motivated and fulfilled.

Applying emotional intelligence to overcome gender-related behaviour in the workplace requires you to:

- recognise how your words and actions impact on others;
- fine tune your listening skills so that you really hear what the other sex is saying;
- make convincing arguments to the other sex in terms they can relate to;

- get better results from mixed-sex teams, who in turn will then have more fun working together;
- earn trust and respect from colleagues and staff and improve working relationships.

Remember: People at work basically want the same things: job satisfaction; the feeling that they are contributing positively to the workplace.

Don't forget that despite the differences between men and women, they have a lot more in common than divides them. If they harness the ability to learn and develop as they carry out their work they will generate positive relationships with their co-workers.

When challenges occur

When leaving highly paid and challenging positions women sometimes give reasons such as a need for more flexibility, a better work–life balance; or wanting to spend more time with their family. However, causes can be linked to an overall lack of job satisfaction and if a woman feels undervalued, overworked or unchallenged in her job it is more than likely due to the culture of the organization. Women are frequently paid less and given less respect than their male colleagues in similar positions within the company. As a result they feel isolated, not part of the 'inner circle' and unable to air their problems with colleagues let alone solve them. The action of leaving the company may take care of the symptoms but does not cure the disease.

Men on the other hand can be keen to create a 'macho atmosphere' at work and many thrive on such challenges. They often fail to see that losing key colleagues costs their company many thousands of pounds in lost revenue. This could be because certain clients may follow the people they like working with; and the inevitable high price involved in recruiting and hiring replacement staff – to name but two.

Can everyone be emotionally intelligent?

Men are equally capable of applying emotional intelligence in the workplace as women. It's just that some women seem to be more naturally geared towards that type of behaviour than some men. It follows therefore that the 'bottom up' business model provides an atmosphere in which women thrive. The men do well too, but some need to acquire new skills.

In the workplace men naturally shift towards the traditional hierarchical working mode. Men's teams have leaders, and a distinct structure, they exist to meet targets. Despite adopting terms such as 'partnership' and 'team-building', men sometimes think a good team player is someone who follows the leader, or the boss's line.

In companies all over the globe there are lots of people unhappy at work. Few workers feel they are getting the opportunity to put their personal strengths and talents to work. Applying emotional intelligence in the workplace helps solve such issues and is one way of unravelling gender differences. It does create a win–win situation – not only for both sexes of employees but for the company as well.

Some common misconceptions

Take for example the common misconception that it is just working women who want to spend more time with their families. This is not a *female* thing – men want it too. Almost everyone – if they were truthful – would admit that they'd prefer to spend less time at work and have more time at home with their loved ones. What everyone at work wants is to feel valued, know that they are making a difference, and gain satisfaction out of the job they do (beyond their pay cheque at the end of the month). There is no gender bias here.

A common misconception is that being equal stands for being the same. It doesn't – men and women don't think in similar ways; they don't communicate in the same fashion; they don't hear the same things when spoken to and they don't mean the same things when they speak.

Emotional intelligence helps to create a positive environment so that people are happy working together. Men and women each have special strengths; knowing how and when to combine those strengths changes the atmosphere in which they work. A healthy working environment (where emotional intelligence has been applied):

- cultivates open and honest communication;
- supports the continual development of all employees;
- recognizes and appreciates everyone's achievements;
- creates trust and values;
- empowers rather than controls;
- encourages an inclusive not an exclusive approach to gender difference;
- promotes individuals' strengths rather than criticizing their weaknesses.

8. Awareness of others

Until he extends his circle of compassion to include all living things, man will not himself find peace.
ALBERT SCHWEITZER (1875–1965)

How aware of others are you? Most of us are guilty of carrying around lots of assumptions and prejudices about other people. You may feel that now the sexes are truly equal, anti-ageism legislation is in force and everyone embraces cultural diversity that this has eradicated any problems. Unfortunately, life isn't that simple and being aware of others is an important part of applying emotional intelligence to decision making and taking action.

The four basic stages

Remember: There are four basic stages of awareness: denial; recognition; puzzlement/disappointment; acceptance/collaboration.

Do you have any idea of how aware you are of others? Does dealing with other people ever become problematic?

Stage One: Denial. This has two forms: unconscious and conscious. The first is when you think you know something, but in fact you don't. The second is when you are aware of something superficially but don't actually understand it.

A remark that shows unconscious denial would be something like: 'There's no problem with the workplace culture, it's just a matter of personality. Anyway, you can't change the way someone behaves.' Someone in denial about awareness of other people will have no problem with their place in the hierarchy; and if they are satisfied, why shouldn't everyone else be too?

An example of conscious denial would be a manager who believes that since there are corporate policies in place at work to deal with certain issues (such as equality, ageism and cultural discrimination), it follows that these cover all problems. Such a person would point to a number of women employees in high-level positions, or cross-cultural teams working together in the company as proof that everything is all right within their corporate world, with little or no regard to whether employees are happy, fulfilled and have job satisfaction. This illustrates that they have some superficial knowledge yet little real awareness of factors affecting others.

Stage Two: Recognition/awareness. This is where, say, a manager realizes that different people perceive things in different ways. In an ideal world everyone would accept the policies laid down and the treatment they are given, and not take issue with the status quo. He might not have realized that one member of staff is thoroughly fed up with his 'sexist comments'. He would not be aware of any problem until it has escalated as far as the HR department who informs him that someone has made a formal complaint about him. However much he wants to 'fix' the problem, he doesn't know how to do so. He falls back on the excuse, 'but this is part of the company culture, staff surely accept it'. He asks the HR manager, 'If there's a problem tell me what I must do, and I'll do it.'

Stage Three: Puzzlement/disappointment. This stage is where the disillusioned manager complains that the company has done everything it can to develop a workable policy; the staff handbook is full of advice for employees on how to avoid escalation of any negative situation. The manager feels that it's not the company but the individual staff member who is at fault. 'Everything has been carefully considered, and the rules are laid down. What else can we do?' Then suggested solutions to the problem are produced along the lines of – what if we employ more young people, less women, recruit people from other cultures. In their frustration, some people revert back to the denial stage, which exacerbates the process.

Stage Four: Acceptance/collaboration. Managers who reach this stage are beginning to see the light. Emotional intelligence is shining through and they become conscious of the workplace being different things to different people, depending on an individual's viewpoint. People who reach Stage Four are aware of others' issues, not just their own. They actively want to change things so that everyone benefits. The enlightened manager announces that he 'wants to make lasting, positive changes within the workplace' and in order to do so empowers his staff to work with him to provide solutions to issues that need addressing. Once the emphasis is placed on creating win–win solutions, the atmosphere improves, communication is clearer and motivation levels are raised. The HR department would be able to report a decrease in staff turnover and an increase in staff performance and output.

Keep on checking

Testing your level of awareness of other people is sometimes painful. Many people struggle with it and it is easy to give up. However, even the most difficult challenges become easier with effort. Once you can see the positive advantages of being people-aware, you should make a determined attempt to keep at it. Ongoing commitment is essential: be ready to look and listen and keep an open mind while doing it. If you find this concept difficult you should work on changing your attitude and behaviour. For example, you know that men and women are equal, but remember that this doesn't make them the same. Knowing that an employee has great technical ability but is weak on interpersonal skills does not mean that this person isn't desirable as a member of staff. It does however present a challenge to the HR department or their line manager to ensure that they work alongside other staff whose own aptitudes are complementary, so that the range of competencies across the department is extended and enhanced.

9. Relationships with colleagues

You can get everything in life you want if you will just help enough other people get what they want.
ZIG ZIGLAR, *SECRETS OF CLOSING THE SALE*, 1984

Getting along with others at work is an important ability to possess. If you find it difficult to relate to colleagues, is this because you are not aware of them, you are nervous or shy, or you don't buy in to the workplace 'culture'? Each organization has a different way of doing things. You need to be able to tune in to the way of talking and acting so as to get the best out of workplace relationships.

Strong feelings of fear, confusion, frustration and overwhelming-ness are common enough when you are starting a new job. Usually by the end of a few weeks things settle down, so it pays to be patient and reserve judgement for a while. The more you learn about the workplace, the more familiar you will become. It may be natural at the end of the first day to go home thinking that every one of your colleagues is an idiot and you'll never be able to cope with that tyrant of a boss. But don't allow such negative emotions to colour everything. It surely couldn't be *all* bad?

Tuning in

One of the best ways to work out how best to relate to colleagues is to watch your co-workers and line manager to see how they do things. Some offices have a fairly relaxed culture and there is no dress code and everyone is greeted on first-name terms. It is always a good idea to check out the rules of the game before you make an embarrassing gaffe that you could have prevented by carefully observing how things happen.

Remember: Colleagues can be challenging. They all have different personalities and some are bound to be easier to work with than others. They may be very different from you, but that doesn't mean they are difficult.

Even if someone says something to upset you, they may not have intended to hurt your feelings. It might simply be their way of doing or saying things. Take a deep breath and allow yourself time to judge what types of characters are in your team or department.

If in doubt, ask

You can always ask questions. One way of getting on with other people is to ask their advice. Few people resent being consulted, particularly if you explain that you value their opinion (because they've had more experience than you for example). If you've recently taken up a new position, you must have been selected because you have something to offer. You need to know how best to use your skills and the only way to find out is by enquiring politely of colleagues or your boss what is expected of you. On the subject of questioning, don't forget an open question will elicit more information than one that requires a 'yes' or 'no' answer. 'Do I put this paper in this file?' won't get you far, but 'Could you show me how you want me to file these papers?' will gain you much more.

When communicating with colleagues, be clear. You want to get your message across in a direct, honest, sincere and positive way. When you are asking for information, be sure to listen very carefully when others are talking to you. If you don't give them your full attention you could miss a vital piece of information and this would be embarrassing if you had to repeat the question. Colleagues can be busy so it is a matter of basic courtesy if they are helping you to pay attention to what they say, and the way they say it.

Not everyone is the same

Colleagues, as has been mentioned, come in all shapes and sizes. Should you come up against criticism or conflict, you must not take things personally. You may need to adjust the way you behave or do your job and telling you is the only way to convey this information. It is not a personal attack; they are explaining that there is something about the way you work that could be improved. If someone criticizes your performance without offering any advice on how to do it better, it is your responsibility to ask for more information. You are not expected to be a mind-reader.

Working requires you to be part of a team. It is rare to find a job that requires no interaction with colleagues. Being part of a group requires certain skills. Try to be a proactive and positive part of a team of colleagues. If you are upbeat and offer suggestions and ideas, colleagues should appreciate that you are interested and willing to help.

Remember: One winning tip is to be enthusiastic with praise. Everyone enjoys recognition and if you are able to tell your coworkers when you like their work, or the way they do things, they will be pleased.

Be aware of other people's boundaries: some people like more space around them, and are private people. It is intrusive if someone stands too close to you in a queue or on the station platform. It is a natural instinct to move away. Should you find that colleagues are withdrawing from you, reflect on your actions and see whether you have invaded their space or overstepped the mark in any way. Should someone get stuck on a piece of work, or is unable to come in due to illness, offer to help out. It will be noted and even if your offer of help isn't taken up, don't hesitate to be helpful when another opportunity presents itself. It will go a long way to show your colleagues that you are caring and aware of other people's situations besides your own.

Of course it goes without saying that unless you feel good about yourself (have a healthy level of self-esteem) you will find it hard to get on well with colleagues. Feeling good, and doing a good job of work is self-motivating. Other people will be much happier to be around you if you have an optimistic and outward-looking personality. Too much introspection narrows thinking and outlook and tends to spread a negative atmosphere around the place. Whether you are negative or positive in outlook tends to come true ('I can do this job well' or 'I'll never be able to learn this'). Which would you prefer?

The more confidence you have in yourself, the more easily you will be able to handle relationships with colleagues.

10. Contrasting personality types – and psychometric tools

Some people are very difficult to read as they do not readily give any emotional cues as to what they are thinking and you get *neither positive nor negative feedback*. This is not easy to cope with as it denies you the chance to establish rapport and inhibits your own ability to communicate easily. In essence, it makes you feel awkward and not certain what to do or say next. In the absence of any clues to the contrary, people may feel that the person in question is stand-offish, uncaring, disinterested or quietly judging you, when none of these may be true.

The cause of the impassivity could be shyness, uncertainty as to how to react or the need to deliberate very slowly. What is certain is that their first instinct is unfortunately not to put you at your ease.

What this demonstrates is that *you cannot not communicate*. Someone will put just as much of an interpretation on your lack of a reaction as to one that is highly apparent. It also demonstrates a lack or suppression of at least one of the five main emotional competencies. It is not, however, an indicator of lower intelligence. In fact, the reverse may be true.

A well-known acquaintance is difficult to have a conversation with because there is always a slight pause before she replies. She is, in fact a shy person and not particularly confident, but others think that she is intellectually arrogant, calculating and manipulative. You could say that she lacks two of the key emotional competencies – awareness of others' emotions and knowing how to influence others' emotions productively. She is, however, highly intelligent and articulate and more appreciative of others and their ideas than they might imagine. She would undoubtedly be surprised at the effect she causes.

As a personality type she is introvert, surprisingly accommodating and conscientious, but outward appearances suggest that she is resistant and closed-minded. To perceive the person she really is needs those with whom she deals to possess a higher degree of emotional competence than usual to perceive the 'person behind the mask'.

By comparison, 'Jack the Lad' – and we all know someone who fits that description – is extrovert, apparently accommodating, apparently open-minded and emotionally uninhibited. He is popular and people think he is great to have around.

However, he is extremely ambitious and manipulative, uses other people for their value to him and not his value to them and has a habit of discarding people when they have served his purpose. Although he is not intellectually gifted, he is very adept at using emotional 'muscle' to make the best of any situation he may be in – and this may see him promoted more quickly than others, more apparently successful in a business environment and also more socially mobile.

What we can see, therefore, is that the link between personality type and intelligence is tenuous. Behind a person's facade is the real him or her; the real values and goals. The relative perception of them is coloured more by emotional forces than intellectual assessment. Gauging such people calls on a well-developed emotional intelligence and, on the one hand to the *toleration of silence (a good emotional skill)* and the ability, perceptively, to read intentions into behaviour.

Between the introvert and the extrovert, positive and negative, are many other shades of personality and these are evidenced in the many psychometric theories and models that are available.

Psychometric tools

You may be in doubt about someone's personality characteristics, or the reasons for the types of behaviours he or she displays, or the interaction between you both or between them and others. You may simply want to be better prepared when conducting an interview or managing your own or someone else's performance and attitudes. Either way, there are many different tools and devices that help you to analyse the type of person he or she might be. Some require a fee to be paid but others are free and can readily be found on the internet.

Many of these psychometric tools are surprisingly reliable (given the speed at which questions can be answered and a diagnosis made) and most people recognize themselves as described in the ensuing reports. However, there should always be caution in regarding them as definitive as there are exceptions to the rule. Generally speaking, these tests are an aid to understanding rather than statements of fact. They would be very good guides when preparing to interview someone or assessing team members as they give you clues to the hypotheses that you might want to examine more closely. A very small sample of those more widely used is given below.

They include the work of Thomas International Inc, which differentiates personality types through the DISC model that assesses the ratios between dominance, influence, steadiness and compliance in order to gauge individuals' suitability for certain job roles. For example, a laboratory researcher would tend to be someone who was steady and compliant with little need to be dominant or influential, whereas a senior director may need to show greater influence.

A useful behavioural and relationship building model is SDI (Strength Deployment Inventory) that contrasts your emotions and behaviour when things are going well compared to when things are going wrong or you may be in conflict with others. By understanding your own motivations you can more easily appreciate why others behave in the way they do. The system uses a three-colour system with shades in between, is easy to use and very accessible.

Not dissimilar in its 'colours' concept is the Insights Learning & Development Discovery Personal Profile that differentiates cautious, competitive, caring and persuasive characteristics (among many others) to show individuals' style, approach, strengths and weaknesses with indicators of where development could take place. These characteristics are represented by four colours, permutations of which extend into eight categories of matching role.

Capitalizing on the categories of personality types described by C G Jung, the Myers-Briggs Type Indicator was developed to make that theory available in a practical way to individuals and groups. Based on four basic personality differences, there are 16 different 'types' that arise from the interaction between them. Having now been in use for many years, the Myers-Briggs Indicator has proved to be very reliable and remains widely used.

Emotional intelligence creates the link between our own and others' feelings and personality orientations. The instruments mentioned above will all help that understanding.

11. Your state of mind reflects both conscious and subconscious feelings

Your mind has both a conscious and subconscious state, each of which has a bearing on how you behave and respond to the different situations around you. Your conscious mind enables you to think, apply logic, calculate and decide. It also enables you to control your emotional response to any given situation and deliberately select from a number of choices.

However, because there is always more sensory information available to you than can adequately be absorbed and processed, the mind filters or summarizes that which it can consciously handle. As everyone is different, this forms their unique map of the world. It may or may not be a realistic representation of things as they really are but is certainly how they are perceived. Nonetheless it is *your* reality and the one that you will have to adjust when communicating with others and their different maps and perceptions.

Your subconscious mind is conditioned and characterized by subliminal experiences. These include irrational fear or dislike (such as of harmless spiders), muscle memory (where your fingers automatically hit the right keys on a keyboard or you can ride a bike, for example), and inexplicable pleasure (such as from taste and music). It is also made up of instinct as well as forgotten incidents and experiences that may have affected your life in the past.

Your values, beliefs and intentions are embodied in both your conscious and subconscious mind, as is your reactive and proactive behaviour. If you have an ingrained aversion to men with beards, or women with beards for that matter, you may be conditioned by both a conscious and subconscious reaction when meeting them.

Your mind is also affected consciously and subconsciously by such stimulants as alcohol, where 'beer goggles' distort how you think and behave, but not necessarily who you are. Some believe that drink reveals the real person, thus the expression 'in vino veritas', which loosely translated means 'when people drink wine *they reveal the truth about themselves*'. The reality is that under the influence of such stimulants your emotions revert to the primal state that we, in common with other animals, are born with. It is the higher layers of our brains (neocortex) that become suppressed and the lower layers (sub-cortex) that predominate.

If you follow the learning cycle that includes both conscious and unconscious competences, it provides a clear illustration of how information progressively gets relegated to the subconscious.

How incompetence can lead to competence

Both conscious and unconscious states of mind can be altered through learning. This is well illustrated through the example of someone learning to drive. When you are planning to have your first driving lesson, you are not conscious of how incompetent you are as you have no idea what you have to do or how to do it. You are *unconsciously incompetent*. As soon as you have been shown how to operate brakes, pedals, steering wheel, gears and mirrors, you are then conscious of your lack of skills in co-ordinating their use. You have become *consciously incompetent*. After several lessons you can be trusted to drive the car, albeit in a faltering way, and you can then be said to be *consciously competent* as you know what to do but still have to think about it while you are doing it. After a while, steering, gear changing and braking are done subconsciously as you have acquired the driving 'habit'. You are now *unconsciously competent*. When you have become unconsciously competent, *it is then that you begin to develop bad habits* such as steering with one hand, using rear view mirrors insufficiently, speeding and so on. It is also the case that you then react spontaneously to emergencies. For example you will swerve or brake to avoid an obstruction in the road without even thinking about it.

The rules by which you run your life comprise both conscious and subconscious elements. Your values may be those you were taught by your family or they may have been influenced in the opposite direction because of your wish to be different. If one of your 'drivers' is punctuality, or honesty, it will probably influence you for life. If you are perpetually late or economical with the truth, you will always have that tendency, even though you can consciously modify your behaviour to change that impression. If you have a tendency to be competitive you are likely permanently to remain so.

Chapter 05
Emotional intelligence and the roles people play

How to be a good leader

CASE STUDY

General Eisenhower, who subsequently became US President, was asked how it was possible to provide effective leadership to so many hundreds of thousands of service personnel. Apparently, as this apocryphal story goes, he took a piece of string from his desk drawer and laid it on the desktop in front of him and said, 'When I push the string in a particular direction, it is not easy to make it go where I want it to. If, on the other hand, I pull it, I can easily take it any way I want.'

This analogy of leadership demonstrates a good understanding of human psychology. If you push people, you are robbing them of an opportunity to decide for themselves that they want to follow and many people resent that. To understand leadership, as compared to management, it is helpful to think of its corollary, which we might well term 'followership'.

Leadership skills can be developed

Leadership implies that people are willing to follow and good leaders have the emotional intelligence to work out what will induce people to do so. As emotional intelligence is not static and can be developed, it follows that leadership skills can also be developed.

Of course, some people are natural leaders. Their personalities, temperaments and ability to communicate are such that they can make people gravitate towards them. Others have to try a bit harder.

If you are perceptive and take the trouble to work out the emotional stimuli that will cause people to want to follow your lead, however reticent you may be, you are well enough equipped to achieve your objective.

Those who 'want to be in charge' usually make it obvious by imposing their views at too early a stage. Sometimes they succeed because of the dominance of their personalities and the fact that others in the group do not want to take charge themselves.

Strength can come from weakness and weakness from strength

A good leader, however, takes responsibility when the time is right and allows others the option of contributing to a decision. Some would say that was a sign of weakness but in reality it is a sign of strength. There is no doubt that, from time to time and in specific circumstances people need direction. However, the emotional intelligence of a good leader is to know when that direction is required and best given.

If you put five human resource specialists who have never met each other into a room together and ask them to define the difference between leadership and management you will most probably hear five different definitions. It will take time to align them all to a common view – assuming that were possible.

Unlikely leaders?

The work of well-known British researcher and management theorist Meredith Belbin into people's relative roles and behaviours within a management team context named one category of individual as a 'Plant'. This person tends to have a high IQ and is introverted but has an ability to be highly analytical and original and can see 'the big picture'. A characteristic of a Plant is that he or she may sit quietly during a discussion that may be being dominated by others in the group. However, at the end the Plant will come up with a 'brilliant' idea or explanation that crystallizes everything that has been discussed. Others in the group then fall in behind because of the seminal contribution that has been made.

In effect, the Plant, without having been the obvious leader of the group, has, in fact, been the ultimate leader of the group. The important qualification is others' preparedness to follow.

Leaders also follow

The titular head of a group need not necessarily be its main leader. This is because anyone from whom others will take their lead can equally well perform that role. The good manager has the emotional intelligence to recognize when someone else in the group can beneficially take the lead (which of itself is a form of passive leadership).

If you are not already familiar with Belbin and his team roles model there are some useful and interesting information sources and additional definitions on the internet.

The perfect team player?

The nickname for former Australian Rugby Union's national team captain, John Eeles, was 'Nobody'. The logic behind this was the saying 'nobody's perfect' and therefore a great compliment to this multi-talented player.

Following on from the above section – anyone can be a good leader – diversity of talent, personality and behaviour can be an advantage to a management team that needs the stretch of different types of input and output. An apposite saying might be, 'if all of us always agree then some of us are unnecessary'.

If all of us always agree then some of us are unnecessary

Rugby Union also provides an excellent analogy for understanding how team performance can be much greater than the sum of its parts.

The front row of a scrum requires strength, weight, power and compactness and front row players are big but not necessarily tall. Behind them, in the second row, are tall, heavy and surprisingly agile players who need to be able to jump as well as push. The back row players need strength, stamina and pace.

Of a different character altogether are those behind the scrum where speed, elusive running, faultless tackling and well-developed ball-kicking skills are important. Sheer size is not so much of an issue.

The effectiveness of the team is in the way that people of different bodily characteristics can work together in an integrated way towards a common goal.

This is not dissimilar to what is required of management teams.

Anatomy of a good management team

The Belbin model has nine distinct behavioural types, each one of which is influenced by personality and, to some degree, by previous experience and aptitudes. Some people will have characteristics that span two or even more of the definitions. The definitions include: a *Co-ordinator* who thinks positively and works well with others; a *Shaper* who tends to be a dominant and assertive influence; a *Resource Investigator* is someone who is always networking and finding things out; a *Company Worker* is a practical and selfless enactor of tasks (that others in the team may not wish to do); a *Monitor-evaluator* is objectively analytical; a *Team worker* makes helpful interventions; a *Specialist* provides expert knowledge and skills; a *Completer-finisher* is someone who can be relied upon to get things done; and a *Plant* is a person who can usually be relied upon to come up with the brilliant idea.

The need for emotional intelligence in a team context is in sensing what you and others are feeling, objectively reviewing the options available to the group and behaving in such a way as leads to the optimum outcome. For this purpose, adjustments have to be made by each individual in his or her communication with others in the group so as to enable movement towards its common purpose. This may mean suppressing some natural behavioural instincts and amplifying others.

On the rugby field, from time to time the smallest person on the pitch may have to bring down the biggest. He may emotionally prefer not to but it's what the team needs.

The secrets of sales success

Compared to the USA where many university graduates will opt for a career in sales (and the majority of top business executives will at some stage of their development have fulfilled a sales role) the UK has never regarded sales as a prestigious occupation. This is evidenced by the surprising fact that sales has seldom been dignified by being on lists of degree courses offered by the mainstream institutions.

Yet successful economic activity depends on trade, and trade depends on people being sold things. So why is there this cultural difference? Part of the explanation could be that the USA has not been encumbered by the British model of social class. 'Trade' in the UK used to have less social status than 'profession'. Universities, until relatively recently, mainly fed the 'professions'.

Why are the British different?

However, other than a general perception in the UK to the contrary – although this may now be changing – there is no reason to suppose that selling is not a profession that can be of similar status to any other. There is certainly no reason why it should not merit a university degree.

Having said that, a pioneering British company, Meta-morphose, was among the first to recognize that high-potential individuals, such as those educated at university, could help significantly to improve the business performance of their employers, provided that they also had the right emotional intelligence. Famous British management guru and broadcasting 'Troubleshooter', Sir John Harvey-Jones was a keen supporter of Meta-morphose's work in converting high-potential graduates into high-performing sales professionals. The effectiveness of these individuals compared to the norm has been impressive.

Emotional factors more important than qualifications?

The emotional factors in selecting the right candidates have, however, been more important than their academic background. It is the combination of the two that has made the real difference. Through assessment days and close observation in behavioural situations, candidates have been singled out against the MERL model that evaluates Motivation, Energy, Resilience and Likeability. Although the latter may in today's parlance sound a little 'fluffy' it is an essential lubricant in the establishment of empathy and rapport.

These graduates are then supported by a programme of experiential (as compared to situational) training to an accredited level during the first and sometimes second year of their employment. Compared to usual success rates for sales recruitment where only 55 per cent are still in the same job after a year, 96 per cent of those trained and nurtured through the one-year programme remain in post and perform well.

High-performing individuals always trump stereotypes

Professions such as teaching, politics, caring, consulting, counselling and HR all need the input of high-potential individuals with well-developed emotional intelligence. Exactly the same is true of sales but, compared to other professions, stereotyping can deter people who might otherwise find a highly motivating and rewarding niche that opens up long-term opportunities for progression.

In any trading situation, there is a clear need to understand the emotional context for both buyer and seller. Only then can trust and rapport be managed. The intellectual capability to match that emotional understanding with an outcome that will have serious value to both parties requires a special talent that can be profitably nurtured and developed in these high-potential individuals. Provided their profession is awarded the status it deserves the economic benefits could be more far-reaching than we currently imagine.

How to sell yourself

There is plenty of advice available on, for example, how to write a compelling curriculum vitae or employment profile, and in this context it can be useful to develop 'An emotionally intelligent CV'. However, it is not easy to generalize when there are so many different types of people on the receiving end of such documents. In some cases, for example, it is suggested that you incorporate a photograph, but depending on how you look and how susceptible the recipient may be to quirks of visual appearance, it may not be the panacea that your advisers have in mind.

In the first instance you will want to know whether your CV will be one of dozens received or one of just a handful. In the former case you will want yours to stand out from the crowd immediately it is picked up. In the second, where you might presume that it would be read more thoroughly, you will want to ensure that the sequence and content of the information provided stands up to a more thorough reading.

In some environments, qualifications are the most important indicator of someone's likely competence in doing a job. If you get to see CVs from Eastern and Southern Europe, for example, the person's qualifications will commonly be the first things you read in the document. In the USA it is now unlikely that if you do not have at least two degrees, one of which is a Masters, you will not get into some of the bigger professional firms.

Experience is important but not necessarily essential

In some organizations, you will not get a job in management unless you have previously had a job in management. This precludes a whole reservoir of excellent talent and limits choice to those who have held a titular position, which, as we know only too well, is not necessarily a good indicator of effectiveness.

On the other hand, enlightened recruiters of sales personnel know that qualifications come second to motivation, energy, resilience and being personable.

So where do you start?

If you think that 'my CV is about me, my abilities and my achievements' that will most probably be the wrong starting point. If, on the other hand you think of the CV as being more about the recipient than you, then you are part-way to a more emotionally intelligent assessment of what is required.

Context is king

The context for providing the CV is also important. If you are sending it as a result of already having had a conversation with the person or people seeking to recruit someone, then the CV is an endorsement of that conversation rather than something that grabs attention for the first time. If the CV is a formality in the process of changing roles in an existing organization, it will be different again. If it is to engage for the first time with someone who does not know you, you will want to create the best possible first impression.

If you think of your CV as a marketing tool, which it is, then marketing rules apply. One of the most important precepts in marketing is that it is about perceptions first and realities second. The primary task is to make an excellent impression rather than just educate the reader – so the emotional appeal is everything.

When less is more

It is very tempting to try to put everything into a CV so as not to sell yourself short. You have a number of choices about how to put it together depending whether you want people to be impressed by your job responsibilities, your achievements, the training courses you have been on, your qualifications or your personal qualities. This means you have to make an assessment as to how the person reading it is likely to react. A CV could be received in the Human Resources department in response to an advertisement or just speculatively, by the prospective manager of the new appointee, a committee or a third-party recruitment organization. Each will be looking to satisfy a slightly different requirement and will wish to be seen to be making a wise judgement on behalf of his or her organization.

The decision on how to sequence and create different emphases in a CV will depend on reconciling your own wish to be seen in the best light with your assessment of how the recipient will react in the most favourable way. The emotional intelligence to be applied is in making that judgement, sometimes against your natural instinct, to achieve the desired outcome.

Passionate or indifferent?

Emotional intelligence is all about being able to interact with other people; using our own emotions in harmony with others' emotions to create a desired outcome.

Success in business and in life comes from our motivation, energy, focus and resilience. Nothing we want is given to us on a plate. Anything that *is* given to us on a plate is less valued than something we have striven to attain. Indifference may do no harm in the short term but may lead to regret over time.

CASE STUDY

In a big UK maritime port many dock-workers' children were educated at the local secondary school. Most fathers believed that they had a job for life and that, when the time was right, they could hand that job down to their sons. Teachers at the school were constantly being frustrated by these sons' attitudes to their schoolwork. The usual argument that it was important to work hard to get anywhere in life was frequently greeted with the response that it was not necessary to do so for those who already had their futures assured in the docks. Any seeds of doubt teachers tried to sow about the wisdom of that assumption were confidently dismissed.

That was in the 1970s and, as we all now know, the big ports were progressively affected by the growth in airfreight and the emergence of container logistics with much less need for human labour.

If you always do what you always did...

Had the boys been more influenced by their teachers than their fathers, been more open-minded about their own abilities and alternative opportunities and motivated to be the best they could, the story may have been different.

Raw intelligence had nothing to do with the attitudes on display; it was the lack of applying emotional intelligence that led to an unsatisfactory outcome.

Anyone who is in what we might call their 'comfort zone' has in-built resistance to venturing outside it. Successful people are those who recognize that creating the temporary discomfort of doing something different, pursuing goals with a passion and being adaptable to circumstances are essential attributes. Indifference need not be a permanent state and, given a positive attitude and will to succeed, emotional intelligence can be enhanced and developed.

'Pilate' decisions lack courage

Quite often in life it is easier to 'wash your hands' of difficult decisions and wait for things to sort themselves out. It is frequently the case in business that managers and leaders defer difficult decisions because they do not want emotionally to face up to them. Doing nothing is almost invariably something that they later regret because they know they should have acted earlier.

Although not a politically correct saying, a nonetheless useful lesson in business is 'If you can't fire them with enthusiasm, fire them with enthusiasm!'

Are there differences between public and private sector management?

There have long been controversial views about the differences between public and private sector leaders, managers and workers. This is not altogether surprising given that there will always be an argument about the tax we pay and what our governments and 'public servants' spend it on.

CASE STUDY

At a British Psychological Society conference some years ago a research paper was presented which confirmed widespread public opinion that civil servants are slower and more bureaucratic compared to private sector managers who are 'sharper and more entrepreneurial'. It went on to say that public sector managers tend to be more serious and cautious intellectual types who like to play with ideas, but are somewhat reluctant when it comes to implementing them. They are more interested in doing things properly, by following processes, procedures and policies, at times at the expense of delivering things quickly. In comparison to private sector managers, they show less sense of urgency and commercial astuteness. Managers in the private sector, on the other hand, tend to be more animated, spontaneous and risk-taking. They focus on results, are pragmatic and more objective and self-assured.

Some people just spend money; others must earn it first

From an emotional intelligence standpoint, what should one conclude from this? It is obvious that there are evident strengths in public sector management behaviour and attitudes yet there are also weaknesses. On the other hand, should there be more done in the private sector to mitigate spontaneity and risk?

At first sight you could judge that the report was pejorative in its representation of public sector management competency and complimentary about private sector management, but would we want more risk-taking and spontaneity in the public sector and less risk-taking and pragmatism in the private sector?

There is no doubt that improvements can be made in both sectors but that we must also value what might by some be considered shortcomings and by others, strengths. What is needed is more sharing of ideas.

The fallacy of a goal-free strategy

CASE STUDY

One of the UK's Regional Development Agencies wanted to create an economic development strategy for the Information and Communications Technology sector. Its managers were asked at a joint agency/industry forum what would be the measurable result of such a strategy in, say, three years' time. The answer was that it is a 'rolling three-year strategy' where measurement would evolve over time.

This is a patently different answer than one that would be given by a private sector manager who would probably have expressed the answer with a numerate outcome. It illustrates a mindset difference between people whose role is predominantly to spend other people's money and those who have no alternative than to earn it. In the case above, the need for numerical measurements was accepted and a committee subsequently set up to determine what the goals would be.

Return on Investment (ROI) measures are notoriously elusive where there is a political consequence to success or failure and there are many different opinions about what success and failure really mean in the first place.

You could argue that it is emotionally intelligent not to put yourself in the firing line, or maybe you are already in the firing line so keeping a neutral profile helps you to operate safely for longer.

Whatever the argument, there are quite clearly differences between public and private sector mindsets, so the question is whether it is important to do something about it or not, and if yes, what should that something be.

On the basis that emotional intelligence is about the alignment and management of feelings and intellect – both ours and the other party's, it would seem obvious that the answer is yes.

Emotional intelligence is more productive

The Regional Development Agency example above demonstrates that it was productive to do so as it resulted in an outcome that was better as a consequence of the meeting of quite different mindsets. Although many organizations support the cultural adoption of emotional intelligence as a means of achieving better performance, it can sometimes be limited to people at an individual level. The real benefit would be for organizations as whole entities to base their decisions on emotionally intelligent management rather than just the expediency of a better HR selection processes.

Why authority wins over status

A parody of the socialist anthem 'The Red Flag' starts 'The working class can kiss my a –, I've got the foreman's job at last', indicating that when people get into positions of greater authority it can sometimes go to their heads.

CASE STUDY

A very personable and talented man joined a business as managing director designate to be made up to the full role after a six-month probationary period. He had gained the enthusiastic support of staff and introduced a number of beneficial changes that meant the company was growing at a faster rate than at any time in its previous history. There was no reason to believe that once in position, this success would not continue.

On assuming the full role things started well enough, but as a 'virgin managing director' there were many additional demands on his energies and it became apparent that he still had a lot to learn about the more stressful aspects of the role. His response was to become autocratic, not, as it should have been in an emotionally intelligent context, more democratic.

Democrats can become autocrats

What had once been influencing skills became coercion, what had been listening skills became rejection of others' views and what had been good control became operational disunity. He prefaced most conversations by referring to his responsibilities as MD and made decisions by virtue of his position and not his leadership skills. Staff attitudes changed to such a degree that when he eventually departed the event was greeted with applause.

This is a very sad story but reflects the not uncommon situation that the position becomes more important than the personality. What had been harmoniously intelligent in one role lost connection with emotional intelligence in the second. Self-awareness and awareness of others' feelings became a problem culminating in the negation of the very talent that had equipped him so well to take up the role in the first place.

Too little confidence?

There are very many people in positions of responsibility who use the position and not their personal competencies to achieve their ends. Often this is because, not of too much confidence, but of too little. The consequence of this is a self-fulfilling process that undermines the respect that others have, makes the job-holder more autocratic and continues the spiral of mutual dissatisfaction.

If you *are* in charge, you don't need to *feel* in charge as you will act the part naturally anyway. Applying emotional intelligence in these circumstances will result in a more outward focus and concentration more on longer term outcomes than short-term respect.

How to solve problems with back-to-front thinking

One way to solve intractable mathematical problems is to consider the extremities of a likely solution before concentrating on the core. Once you know the extremities, you know that the answer is somewhere in between, you have a starting point and can then proceed with the process.

CASE STUDY

One company was reviewing its three-year strategy and was keen to improve its service levels and quality processes. One of the directors said that before knowing what to aim at they needed to know 'what "good" looks like'.

This is a perfectly reasonable premise on which to start and a common device to get people focused on an outcome. It is, however, harder to do and likely to lead to long debatable lists that then have to be vetted and prioritized – in other words a fairly arduous and sometimes contentious process.

The other extreme is 'what does "bad" look like?' – which may sound perverse but is often easier to do. This is because 'bad' paints a picture that everyone can imagine easily because it causes a definite and specific emotional response. 'Good' on the other hand, is the normality that everyone wants to achieve. Normality is likely to be more bland and therefore harder to envisage. It is easier to work from bad to good than imagine every conceivable manifestation of 'good' before you start.

Religious denomination – divisive or inclusive?

CASE STUDY

This is a true story about a Methodist and a United Reform church in talks about merging into one. It was no longer viable for each of these churches to continue on its own and there were local building and planning issues that precipitated the need for talks. The reasons for getting together were economically sound but there was a lot of argument about compromising the different long-established traditions and beliefs that each congregation espoused. For every compromise idea put forward there were many more objections. Repeated meetings did little to resolve the impasse.

Reaching agreement looked as if it would be very difficult until someone said 'What are the good reasons for NOT merging?' at which point there was immediate consensus that there were hardly any at all. This changed the mindset of the meeting so that instead of constantly finding objections to points of detail, there was very quick agreement that 'We should go ahead anyway'.

The 'no alternative' alternative

The emotional preoccupation with problems was converted to an emotional commitment to a solution that everyone wanted. In effect it was emotional intelligence (with or without divine intervention!) that won the day.

Some would say that what we are showing is lateral thinking, which it is. Emotionally intelligent decisions should not just be based on the obvious options but also those that may not previously have been considered. Back-to-front thinking is just one device.

When experts override emotional intelligence

Many people rely on experts but every so often there are news stories that reveal some expert opinion as having more to do with ego than emotional intelligence.

So-called 'experts', who use their training and qualifications as a means of giving themselves authority rather than winning that authority and trust, may be less effective than those with the emotional intelligence to develop more mutually productive relationships.

This can sometimes be the case in the medical profession, for example, when patients who might otherwise be confident and assertive, subjugate that attitude to the clinician's temporarily superior position. These days, medical training includes positive ways of communicating with patients so that they in turn maintain a positive rather than subservient frame of mind. Although things are now much different, there are still many cases where a divide exists and patient feelings are treated as less important than the clinician's social superiority.

It's all about attitude

In predicting someone's likely effectiveness as an employee, or even as an adviser, there is need to consider skill, knowledge and experience as well as qualifications. However, the most important consideration of all is contained in the word 'attitude'.

If the emotional state of the individual is positive and motivated, then any other barriers can be overcome. If the emotional state is negative, there will be less willingness to make changes to the status quo because of lack of belief that anything will be made different.

There is no doubt that we need experts but there is also no doubt that they are more effective when applying emotional intelligence in pursuit of the results they want.

Chapter 06
The evolution of an emotionally intelligent organization

The use of emotional intelligence as a corporate tool

Apart from its use in the selection and personal development process, emotional intelligence also has a powerful role to play in the development of culture and performance in the organization as a whole.

Stephen Covey in *The Seven Habits of Highly Effective People* refers to 'producers' as compared to 'managers' in an organization and the relative effects of telling people what to do next compared to the results that are expected from them. He describes the first as 'gofer delegation' and the second as 'stewardship delegation'. It is the latter category that is most effective in producing results.

Command or encourage?

Those with the 'gofer' mentality, he says, are likely to say 'go for this, go for that, do this, do that, and tell me when it's been done'. Those with the stewardship approach will take the time and trouble to achieve mutual understanding. They will help the person to whom work is being delegated to understand the desired goals, to identify the parameters, to be equipped with the right resources, to know the standards required in order to evaluate results and appreciate what the consequences could be for good or unsatisfactory performance.

The value of investing in people

Analogous to this approach is the UK-originated Investors in People (IiP) standard. This is designed to simplify an approach to management that identifies and promotes strategies for improved organizational performance. It sets out actions to improve that performance and evaluates the impact on the organization.

It involves those at the top of the organization – the 'Top Team' – its operational management and the people who work in it to help achieve its goals.

A good, if slightly sentimental, illustration of the link between performance and an enlightened management approach comes from a long time ago when Lyndon Johnson had become US President following the assassination of JF Kennedy. Apparently, he was on his way by cavalcade to the rocket launch station at Cape Canaveral when he stopped his car next to a man who was sweeping the road to the launch pad. On being asked why he was sweeping the road, the man replied 'I'm helping to put a man on the moon, sir'.

Importance of the big picture not just the detail

If this is indeed a true story it illustrates the connection between even quite menial tasks and a big corporate goal and the commitment engendered by giving someone a clear sense of belonging, recognition and purpose.

The IiP standard envisages 10 things. The first four are to do with strategy and broadly include:

- a clear definition and shared understanding of the parameters for the performance improvement of the organization;

- a plan that links learning and development with organizational objectives;

- an approach to managing people that embraces fairness and equality of treatment;

- a clear set of requirements for managers.

The second four are about the action to be taken and include:

- tangible evidence of effective leadership;

- evidence that people's contribution to the business is valued and recognized;

- people can endorse that they take ownership and are empowered in the decision-making process;

- learning and development is shown to take place.

Finally, there are the key outcomes to be measured:

- the causal link between the investment that has been made in the development of people and the organization's performance as a whole;

- evidence to support improvements that have been made and will continue to be made as a matter of policy.

Investing in 'emotional capital'

Investors in People predates emotional intelligence but anticipated the need to link the way people feel and are treated with the way they link both practically and emotionally with their organizations.

It would have been invented years previously had it been understood that the impact of building 'emotional capital' was as important as the systems, processes, products and financial decisions that also drive an organization's success.

The people-orientated approach had to displace what was a traditional or emotional inclination to treat people as essential cogs in a mechanism in which it might be risky to allow them to think for themselves. The emotional intelligence has been in recognizing that the deferred gratification which comes from developing people provides significantly greater rewards in the longer run.

Prepare for a longer race

An organization that does not put people first could be seen to have, in the extreme, much in common with a Fascist state or fundamentalist movement that suppresses thought, discourages intellectuals and expects people to follow without question. In the short term that may work but in the longer term develops the weaknesses of its strengths. Enlightened managers develop the strengths of people's weaknesses, so that they can convert to significantly better performance and can become permanently better equipped both emotionally and in the practical execution of their roles.

Emotional factors in organizational change

'Eighty per cent of strategy is never implemented' according to the originators of the Balanced Business Scorecard. Too often there are broken links between the strategists and other parts of the business. The strategic intent may not have filtered down to the shop floor, sales staff, production management, service departments and so on. A vision of the future, in this regard, is no good unless it is shared.

In smaller businesses, many owners and managers say that there is never time to take the strategic view. They are far too busy. If they are always too busy and 'do what they always did', they will 'always get what they always got'. How to extricate themselves and their organizations from this predicament is a challenge, not just to their management of time, but also to their emotional intelligence.

To make sure that change happens needs the right number of things to be in place at the right time. There also needs to be a 'commonality of language' (to avoid ambiguities).

You will need to check:

- alignment of different people's priorities (to see the strategy as a whole);
- preparations for change have been made;

- that the change is being managed as it happens;
- that it works, is proportionate and every part is totally relevant for the future;
- that you have discarded any 'unnecessary baggage'.

If you ensure that others in the business are involved, because they know what is going on in the business, you will then be able to trust them. Also, you will need to check out everyone's impact on each other (the knock-on effects or potential unintended consequences). Do also recognize the difference between involvement and commitment and cultivate the latter.

As a consequence of the change, the following checklist will help you to ensure that the emotional as well as the practical outcome is positive and leads to practical improvements.

Board-level ambiguity

If colleagues compete for their views to predominate then those below them will be confused. If they converge and present a united front then those below will be motivated by clear messages rather than demotivated by those that are imprecise or ambiguous.

Leadership

Whether it comes from the titular leader(s) or not, there has to be a 'champion' who lives and embodies the new 'vision'. If everyone is supposed to be responsible, but no one in particular is responsible, there will be a dissipation of focus, effort and achievement.

One goal

There has to be a clear and sustained purpose to which people can commit. It should be easily understandable and able to inspire at all levels in the organization.

Clarity of intention

There has to be a clear reason why the changes in culture and attitude have to take place or else inertia can set in or, as is frequently the case, dictatorial behaviour can unfortunately kick in.

The illusion of harmony

Don't expect everyone to back the changes, but don't stoop to the lowest common denominator of agreement either. You need the stimulation of sceptics who will either be right or force a repeated re-evaluation of the adopted changes.

How candid should you be?

Tell people as much as you reasonably can. Take some risks with candour – this is likely to work better in an organization whose change delivers growth rather than one facing adverse circumstances.

Communication

Effective communication is essential and almost impossible to overdo. Communication links can, however, break down in stressful situations due to being given inadequate priority. Uncertainty and major change create anxieties that must be dampened if morale and performance are not to deteriorate.

Senior people must take more responsibility

The more senior you are, the more responsibility you need to take. Every top management action sends a signal. Delegation should not translate as abdication if a strategic change is to progress properly.

Empowerment is not always absolute

Even enterprising employees need leadership. The wider experience and vision of senior personnel gives them a co-ordination and leadership role that those below should be able to count on.

Teams and leaders

Good teams and good leaders support each other. Teams often contain hierarchies of power and responsibility. Senior people may not lead the team but they have a powerful sponsorship role in the organization.

Structure and culture

Use structure to change culture. It is normally easier and faster to change the structure, reward and measurement systems and the performance criteria that will create longer term effects than to try to redesign directly to achieve a 'quick fix' cultural change.

Creating winners

Personal success is a great motivator but an autocratic regime fosters risk aversion and a blame culture. It is better to recognize meritorious failure as well as success to show that all those in the organization are properly valued.

Fast change and initial acts

Early successes create productive momentum. There should also be intermediate milestones of achievement that raise people's confidence in their ability to succeed further. Speedy successes (or quick wins), even in relatively minor matters, demonstrate purpose and commitment.

Caring for casualties

Caring for people, as well as being morally commendable, is organizationally effective. The worse you treat those who are no longer valued enough, the more resistance to change will grow. Survivors will adopt defensive strategies in case they may be next.

Minimizing unintended consequences

You cannot avoid all errors, but you can organize yourself to anticipate some and recover from others. Mainly this will be to do with contingency resources that a well-thought-through plan can allow for.

In managing a change project, ensure that you get responses from all viewpoints, not just one. Many change projects fail because, for example, IT projects are considered as IT projects and not the business-change projects that they really are. It is also worth asking customers the changes that they might suggest (and get them to share, or even pay for, the cost of those changes).

All change should be based on fact and not assumptions. The changes will be faster the more that people are involved in the vision and the process. It is their emotional commitment that outstrips the practical measures and that will be sustained if people are treated well.

When small improvements can create big gains

If a principal aim of a commercial organization is to create profit, whatever that profit might subsequently be used for, it will do so not just by one but a number of means. It is the collective organization and use of money, management and marketing that will lead to its success. However effective the organization has become, it is likely always to be seeking continuous improvement, or else its competitors might do better.

It can be tempting to think that substantial improvement comes from big decisions and organizational changes, and from time to time those are necessary. It is also the case that a larger number of small improvements can have a dramatic impact on the company's fortunes and, in particular, its profits.

Following the idea that a number of small gains can be better than one big one is the model below (Table 6.1). It looks at the basic performance objectives that an organization might have, the activities used in managing the business and specific areas where decisions will have an impact on profitability. The decisions are not necessarily radical but cumulatively can have an exponential effect.

TABLE 6.1 Productivity improvement matrix

PERFORMANCE OBJECTIVES	ACTIVITY FOCUS	SPECIFIC DECISION AREAS	% GAIN NEEDED	PROFIT IMPACT
Generate income	Marketing programmes New name sales Account development Price/contribution levels Discounts and incentives	Market definition Product/service suitability Product/service proposition Segmentation Targeting and timing Incentive programmes Selling/negotiating skills		
Control costs	Purchasing effectiveness Use of materials Operating decisions Negotiation	Wastage of resources Fixed costs Discretionary costs Overheads Negotiating skills Expenses Time costs		

TABLE 6.1 *Continued*

PERFORMANCE OBJECTIVES	ACTIVITY FOCUS	SPECIFIC DECISION AREAS	% GAIN NEEDED	PROFIT IMPACT
Use people intelligently	Clear business goals	Measurable objectives		
	Organization structure	Skills and knowledge		
	Roles and responsibilities	Time		
	Flow of information	Effort and competence		
	Resource planning	Communication		
	Evaluation/training	Motivation and attitude		
	Pay and incentives	Efficient processes		
		Learning		
Use assets efficiently	Depreciation	Capacity and utilization		
	Gearing	Efficient deployment		
	Interest levels	Fit for purpose		
	Stock	Maintainability		
	Capacity	Purchasing policy		
	Utilization	Replacement policy		

TABLE 6.1 *Continued*

PERFORMANCE OBJECTIVES	ACTIVITY FOCUS	SPECIFIC DECISION AREAS	% GAIN NEEDED	PROFIT IMPACT
Manage cash wisely	Credit control Reduction of borrowings Investment policy	Product/service performance Warranty Billing efficiency Cash collection/debtor days Time period efficiency Banking utilization Speed of cash to bank		
Ensure strong intangibles	Quality Reputation Goodwill	Right first time Customer relations Public perception Good culture, values, attitude and brand		

In the column '% gain needed', the question should be asked 'by what percentage could we improve effectiveness in each of the areas shown?' The minimum starting point should be 1 per cent. The emotional connection to this is that it would be very unlikely for anyone to say that productivity could not be improved by just 1 per cent in each of at least 30 of the areas. One per cent is not emotionally challenging and is easy to agree with. If 10 per cent improvement had been asked for in each of 30 cases then that would be considered a challenge too far and beyond the capability of any emotional investment.

You can calculate how much you could make

If performance were improved by 1 per cent in each of 30 areas, the multiplier effect would be significantly greater than the sum.

If this hypothesis is modelled it will not be difficult to envisage figures such as 50 per cent profit improvement: a substantial gain by any standards.

In reality, some of the areas could be improved by substantially more than 1 per cent. Simply by cutting waste, reducing overhead costs, better use of time and reducing mean time between product or service failure could have an immediately measurable benefit.

Why not look at the table and look at those areas where you would be fairly certain that percentage improvements could be made in your own line of business. Would you or your organization commit to achieving that?

From an emotional intelligence perspective, it is easier to invest time and energy in something that is perceived to be easy. It is like the challenge of eating an elephant, which of course is impossible but becomes more reasonable when you break the task down into bite-size chunks.

How to give your business a sporting chance

Sports and business psychology can be surprisingly similar. This was the conclusion from a cross-section of business and professional people who were asked to explore parallels between the two. The same characteristics that make people and teams win at sport are found in successful management teams as well as among leaders and entrepreneurs. To win, a sportsperson not only needs to have the knowledge of the game and the skill to execute a competent performance but also the emotional competencies in terms of self-awareness and awareness of an opponent's frame of mind, whatever the outward appearances.

There's no better example of the need for emotional 'edge' than tennis. How is it that, despite a well-developed set of skills, a tennis player can lose the first set of a match by 0–6 and win the second by 6–2? His or her ability is the same in both sets but it is mental attitude and qualities such as confidence, determination, competitive spirit, together with some occasional luck, that make the difference. Most important of all is the player's adaptability to the situation faced.

From hundreds of ideas and suggestions emerged a consensus on the most important and relevant points, listed below.

Clear goals and winning strategy

If you do not have a crystal-clear purpose how can you select the best means of achieving it? Every team and every business needs a game plan.

A mental picture of what success looks like (visualization)

Imagining what it feels like to win provides impetus and confidence and removes doubt in a sportsperson and is akin to the 'Vision' that provides clarity and motivation in an organization.

Adaptability to different or changing circumstances

As those who play outdoor sport know very well, the weather can have all sorts of effects on the outcome. The future, in this regard, is never quite what you might expect. One definition of the future is that 'it comes sooner than you think and not in the order you expected'. It is you and those in your organization who control reaction to changing circumstances and how to adapt to them.

Meticulous planning

If you fail to plan, you are planning to fail. Forensic attention to detail and consistent application of a good diet of standards, processes and policies will result in a fit, properly fed body that is ready for the challenge.

Self-belief and belief in the team

If you do not trust yourself you will not trust others. If you do not trust others you will never improve.

Determination to succeed

Your desire to win is ultimately more important than your ability to win.

Confidence in own ability, strengths and competitive strategies

If you are too modest and reasonable, your competitors and your customers won't be!

Pride in presentation/turnout

Scruffy is not the same as relaxed and laid back. See yourself through others' eyes. Their perception of you and your brand is more important than any reality.

Ability to step back and see the 'view from the terraces'

If you get lost in a jungle, the best solution is to climb a tree. You've been so busy working hard, you may be somewhere entirely different from what was planned and now need to adjust your strategy.

Preparedness to seek outside advice and support

You don't necessarily have to take others' advice, but if you do not seek it you are robbing yourself of the opportunity for an objective reality check. It will help *you* decide with more confidence whether you are, or are not, in the right lane or even on the right track.

Use huge energy but stay simultaneously relaxed

If you have tight shoulders your golf swing will be lousy and lack power, however much effort you apply. The key is to focus energy on specific areas rather than dissipate it in unproductive use of time and effort.

Positive v negative mindset (expect the best – get the best)

When you have a half-time drink you will enjoy it more if the cup is half full. If you think it is half empty, that disappointment will affect your attitude for the second half and you will be deprived of the energy you need.

Be pragmatic – never take things personally or beat yourself up

If you have the ability to succeed and others sometimes express their doubts or disapproval, keep going and win through. If you are doing the right thing (but not always doing things right) you will invariably succeed.

Be clear about your and competitors' strengths and weaknesses

If you win a match by just one point you are still champion and your competitor isn't. Satisfy yourself that you can win and do it. You don't necessarily have to 'thrash' the opposition at all times.

Focus, focus, focus

Two pistols blazing from the hip are less effective than one pistol properly aimed even though that might look less exciting in a Western movie. It is why karate black belts can chop through seemingly unbreakable piles of bricks. A business with a clear focus will always beat a business that is all things to all people.

Of the above, it is mainly the human factor that makes the difference between superior and merely average performance. Anyone leading a sporting endeavour, as well as anyone leading people in a work environment, should be considering not just the mechanical or operational dimensions but the emotional response and judgements that drive the best of physical and team action to produce the optimum result.

Chapter 07
Emotional intelligence blind spots

The emperor's new clothes – or clever psychology?

CASE STUDY

One of the world's most powerful and influential computer companies wanted to launch a package of accounting software for its distribution partners to resell. It believed that, with its own brand name behind it, the market would embrace it as an important competitor to the other well-established third-party packages being bought in volume at that time.

A launch event was held at a London location and putative resellers were invited to learn about the product and of the marketing campaign that would kick-start its market entry.

Expensive glossy brochures had been designed and printed and each delegate was given a holdall, folders and other gift items to mark the occasion. Part of this pack included details of an advertising schedule in the national quality daily press.

The substance of this was a single insertion of a whole-page advertisement in each of the three leading daily broadsheet newspapers. The declared expectation was that this would create awareness and demand for the product so that resellers would have a good platform from which to sell the software to their prospective clients.

Big statement, minimal effect?

For some people in the room this raised a few eyebrows as it used the whole of the marketing budget available, apart from that needed for some additional sales literature or which had already been spent on the London launch. The question was whether just three advertisements, irrespective of being either whole pages or not and in quality newspapers or not, could possibly make an impact on the market.

Although this launch predated the introduction of emotional intelligence as a concept, the decision that had been taken did call into question the sense of such an advertising strategy.

Was it to do with the perpetrators or their audience?

What of course we cannot gauge was whether the campaign had been devised to impress the resellers or to impress the market; whether there was hidden wisdom behind what otherwise seemed a frankly daft idea. We may never know.

A decade or so later and there has never been any evidence of market adoption. Indeed it is doubtful whether the product still exists – so was this poor marketing, a less than impressed reseller community or change of commercial strategy?

This example provides a relevant case study for emotional intelligence. The emotional assessments that had to be made should have taken account of the market acceptability of yet another accounting product, the resellers' belief that it would be worthwhile selling it, the extent and quality of response from the market and the longer term strategy for the product's promotion.

Success is about deciding on the best choices

There were plenty of choices available to the company in the way it could have launched the product, engaged with the resellers and ensured their commitment to selling it. They decided to 'blow the budget' on what they thought would make a big impression but the outcome failed to live up to expectations.

Arguably, lessons will have been learned by the episode and certainly they will have included the need to take account of understanding their own emotions, the emotions of their resellers and the lack of any logical or emotional impact from the marketplace.

Doomed from the start?

From the perspective of cognitive intelligence alone the strategy did not stack up. If you add the emotional quotient, it could never have done.

What we suspect is that a particular individual or department was given the responsibility for implementing 'the good idea' of establishing a revenue stream through selling packaged software to support its other activities. What we also suspect is that those who gave the instruction to do it had not engaged the emotional brains of those who had to implement it. They in turn completely lacked the knowledge with which to take the product to market and the emotional reasoning capacity to question how best it should be done.

Retail therapy – but not as we know it

CASE STUDY

A well-known retail stores group, in order to maximize the returns from every individual shopping on its premises, enjoins its staff to ask all customers a set of questions designed to stimulate additional purchases. Everyone on every visit to every till must be asked if he or she would like a plastic carrier bag, help with packing, would like to sign up to the store's credit card and would like to purchase chocolate or other special offer 'temptation'.

The company also runs regular till checks on its staff and marks them down if they do not ask all the questions. They are then checked again on a future occasion to find out whether they have improved.

Although for some individuals on the staff they are prepared to ask all of the questions all of the time, for others it causes them stress because they would prefer to use their judgement in creating rapport with the customer.

Know your customer

This was not the only retailer to use the method. It was noted, not long ago in the press, that customer satisfaction at another retail group's outlets had seriously deteriorated. The anecdotal reason was that emotional pressure was being put on staff to put emotional pressure on customers who were fed up with being asked questions.

This flies in the face of an emotionally intelligent approach which calculates that happy and motivated staff will automatically look after customers' interests if they themselves are being treated similarly.

Think about emotional response

Transactions with customers, because buying is an experience, not merely a process, is made more enjoyable and productive if both sides to the transaction can communicate freely if they want to. In the same way that it is futile to demand an apology because you will never know whether it is really meant, it is pointless to create an artificial communication just because you are told to do it.

Recognizing the 'rictus smile'

Physically, we are unable to disguise an artificial smile just as we cannot disguise a real one. There are entirely different sets of muscles at play.

It is therefore emotional manipulation to expect people to smile, ask genuinely interested questions, and offer to help if they are doing it because they are told to and not because they want to.

More enlightened stores tell their staff not to ask customers about things they believe they will not be interested in; to use their judgement and to enjoy customer interaction but to look for genuine opportunities to deliver additional benefit. That is both motivating and empowering.

Retail therapy in this context is what the retailer and not what the customer really needs.

Chapter 08
Persuasiveness
in business

The emotionally intelligent art of persuasion

The cornerstone of persuasion is trust. If you are not trusted, there is no reason why anyone should go along with what you say. Before you pass first base, you will have to take conscious steps to win trust.

Sadly, this is not just the art of an honest person but is also used by dishonest manipulators to achieve the outcome that they, rather than you, most desire. A truly trustworthy person will take pains to provide evidence to support a case, whereas a dishonest one will skilfully steer you away from genuine corroboration.

The power of admitting a negative

One way to win trust is to admit a fault or to provide the bad news as well as the good. This gives the listener the cue for more questions to satisfy him or herself as to the validity of the person providing it. From an emotional intelligence perspective, what is happening is a displacement of a natural instinct not to admit a negative and replace it with a considered statement that demonstrates openness and is thus more likely to lead to a better outcome in the long run.

The emotionally intelligent persuader knows that being able to assess the downside risk in any proposition gives comfort and confidence that there will be a balanced rather than skewed platform for a decision.

Advice robs people of their status

One thing designed to impair the persuasion process is to give advice. Advice robs people of their status and puts the adviser in the emotional ascendancy, whether that was the intention or not. However well-meaning, when you observe people being given advice when they did not ask for it, you can see their hackles rise.

The less you say and the more you listen, the more persuasive you will be. People like to talk because they think that by doing so they are being persuasive. They believe that giving reasons to agree, providing statistics to back their argument and making it seem unthinkable that anyone could reject the superiority of their position is effective persuasion. In fact the reverse is true.

The power of anecdote

A more effective technique is to deflect direct emotional involvement by referring to what someone *else* has done or thinks. In that sense, like other emotionally intelligent tactics where you 'move the goalposts' and change, for example, the context of the proposition, people's emotional positions will be neutralized.

CASE STUDY

An opportunity arose for a company to provide Strategic Account Management training to a client who believed there could be improvements to their business if they did so. They asked the company to say how it would deliver such training and what it would include. A suggested programme was sent. It was quite detailed and, although it contained much of what was expected, did not fire the client's imagination sufficient for him to say 'yes'. The programme was then revised and resent and an affirmative answer received.

The question is whether taking the literal interpretation of this request would be as effective as thinking about it in a different way. The person making the request should maybe have highlighted the issue as a problem to be solved rather than as a training 'product' to be delivered. The person responding to the request should maybe have deflected that request in favour of getting the client talking about his customers in more detail and what results were wanted through better engagement with them.

Question yourself as well as others

If you were to ask the question 'what is my client more interested in? Is it his customers and what might be earned from them or is it my training product?', the answer is that he would probably have a more animated and productive conversation about the former than the latter. Just by talking about those customers and their characteristics would lead to an alignment of thought that would confirm the supplier's empathy towards and understanding of what needs to be achieved. The emotionally intelligent 'trick' is to get the people you want to persuade talking freely about what most interests them. That is to say, creating the focus on where the value comes from rather than just the tool needed to create it.

Verbal armoury is also important, particularly so when it serves to simplify and clarify. A well-chosen word or phrase can communicate a point succinctly when double the number of words will obscure it or add the possibility of ambiguity or misrepresentation. A further impediment to good communication is generalization and it is always very tempting to talk about how capable, flexible and committed we are – which is exactly the same as other suppliers will be saying. What we really want to do is to isolate what is relevant and directly specific so listeners can focus on something concrete rather than abstract.

'Specific' is usually better than generalization

Although it has nothing to do with persuasion but everything to do with good leadership, a true story from John Caines' *The Effective*

Entrepreneur illustrates the powerful effect of being specific rather than general.

CASE STUDY

The managing director of a national house-building firm was making a Friday visit to one of its development sites. He could have asked the site manager 'how are things going?' This would have been a common but general question to ask and would probably have elicited the response 'Not so bad, thanks', which would have been an inconsequential answer to an inconsequential question. However, the question he did ask was 'What was the last complaint you had?' This is a specific question that requires a specific answer.

Homing in on the reality

In this instance, it turns out that it was a problem with a bathroom tap. The next and really quite obvious question to ask is 'Is that just an isolated complaint or have there been others like that?' In this case it turned out that bathroom taps presented quite a frequent problem. On checking by phone with other site managers, it also turns out to have been even more widespread. As a consequence, all the site managers were instructed to come in the following day, irrespective of it being the weekend, to ensure that the tap problem was fixed for all new homes on all new sites. It was a non-negotiable instruction. The problem was duly resolved.

The consequences of being non-specific would have cost the company time, materials, money, customer satisfaction and its reputation.

'Lend me your ears'

Famous quotations are remembered because they are succinct and immediately relevant to situations with which we can all associate. They may also be more memorable because they express some kind of challenge or incongruity. Persuasion also depends on this kind of impact, so it is emotionally intelligent to weigh the effect of every word and phrase on the result you want to achieve.

Emotional intelligence and marketing

There is no better manifestation of emotional intelligence than successful marketing. The corollary of this is that unsuccessful marketing is the consequence of paying too little attention to reason and emotion, both of which are needed if people are to be persuaded along a particular path.

Marketing is essentially a battle of perceptions, not of facts. Why else, for example, would someone buy a branded pack of headache pills when there are unbranded packs of an identical product at a tenth of the price? The answer is that the branded product is *perceived* to be better; it has created a feeling of confidence.

Perception is more important than reality

CASE STUDY

A British company whose founders produced a very high-quality range of pressé drinks using only the most pure of ingredients, were brilliant at producing the product but less well-equipped to understand the finer arts of drinks marketing. As a consequence they brought in a marketing specialist with particular experience in drinks retailing.

Although a number of stores were stocking these drinks, they were selling them at a price that was well below what one would describe as other 'luxury' products. One of the dilemmas faced was that these products were not selling in sufficiently high volume to create the returns necessary to justify further expansion. This then begged the question about pricing. Were the products not selling enough because their pricing was too high, because the stores were not merchandizing them effectively, or what?

Counter-intuitive but successful

As in many situations like this, the answer was counter-intuitive. Instead of lowering prices, they were raised to the level of other luxury drinks and as a consequence were then displayed, not with the cheaper drinks as they had been previously by the stores, but alongside their more prestigious counterparts. The consequence was that sales immediately went up and product profitability increased as well. Production capacity was then increased and the product has now become a well-respected national brand.

The marketing strategy introduced by the new marketing – and later, managing – director had the impact of changing both the commercial buyers' and the public perception of the product. Although it was factually the same, its emotional capital and the perception of its value were significantly enhanced.

The choices

Alternative options that could have been considered to increase sales might have included a big increase in the marketing budget (for which money would have to have been borrowed), to employ a bigger sales force, to change the packaging and various other tactical moves. The natural inclination might have been to do these and certainly not raise prices. The actual decision was much more emotionally intelligent than that and now many more people are benefiting from a product and a business that has made a bigger economic and social impact than could ever previously have been envisaged.

Value propositions and their importance in satisfying customers

A not uncommon failing perpetrated by marketers who are not fully in touch with the emotional agenda of potential customers, is to focus on products and services much more than they do on the emotional context of a transaction. The expression 'value proposition' is often just seen as describing features and benefits, but in reality encapsulates a range of emotions and motivations. The logic of this is explained using the diagram in Figure 8.1.

FIGURE 8.1 The emotional framework of a purchase decision

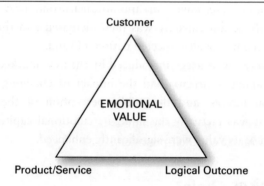

When a customer purchases a product or service it is with the purpose of achieving a logical outcome. There may be a number of products or services that could achieve a similar outcome, but the customer has to make a choice.

The question to ask is 'what value does the customer perceive in using this product or service to achieve that outcome?'

Imagine that the product in question is a bottle of perfume. The logical answer is that it will make you smell more fragrant than if you had not used it. The emotional answer could be quite different. Apart from maybe liking one smell better than another, its value may be in making you more confident in a room of people. It may be to make yourself more attractive to your partner, or to give the impression that you have good and expensive taste. In a practical sense, it may be that, given that you have an ailment, it is the best fragrance to disguise the smell of perspiration. Whatever the motivation, the most important value is in how it makes you feel and not what it is.

Understanding the subtlety of context

If it is someone else buying the perfume for you as a gift, the value to them is not in the intrinsic merits of the product but the effect it creates as a gesture. You would want to buy the one that made the recipient most valued. 'Joy', proclaimed as the most expensive perfume in the world, would convey a very clear message of worth to someone who was given it as a present. A department store's own brand, although you might buy it yourself because of cost, would not be appreciated in the same way if it were given to you as a token of infinite love!

Once, when asked what business it was really in, a perfume manufacturer said that it was 'hope'.

This raises a number of marketing questions about other products and services and positioning them so as to maximize competitive advantage for their providers.

What value a hole?

For instance, a well-known company manufacturing electric drills many years ago, would have responded to the question 'What business are you in?' by saying 'drills' – which seems completely logical. Taking that a step further and asking the question 'What are electric drills for?' elicited the answer 'for making holes'. The final question, 'What are those holes for?' subsequently drew the answer, 'for attaching things to surfaces in the home or other objects'.

Although they may seem contrived answers they are both strategically and emotionally important. When the company was just manufacturing drills, all it could do was to continually improve the product. When it widened the description to include holes it was able to introduce other, different product lines that complemented the range. When it became part of the fixings business, it could extend its line even further to accommodate a whole new range of home improvement products. It is now a home and garden improvements company that is very successful and has captured the mindshare of a whole market.

Emotional perceptions rule

As illustrated, marketing is very much about adjusting your own and your market's emotional perceptions and using emotional intelligence to produce results that exceed original expectations.

Negotiation – an ideal opportunity to demonstrate emotional intelligence

Negotiation, by its nature, needs an emotionally intelligent approach so as to achieve a desired outcome. The reason people negotiate is that there is a mutual intention to achieve something in the interests of both parties. Unless the intention exists in both, you cannot negotiate.

Each party has to be able to read the emotions of the other so as to know what drives them politically, technically and emotionally, and what will cause both favourable and unfavourable reactions. However, negotiators, like poker players, never want to reveal their hand all at once.

Negotiation is, in effect, a collaboration, and its purpose is to lead to mutually acceptable results. Because it is collaborative, it is important for each negotiator to retain a neutral stance. If one party or the other tries to be too dominant it is unlikely to lead to real negotiation. You can only negotiate effectively if you have freedom of movement and choice to propose and decide.

Understand the other's mindset

In a sales negotiation, different mindsets are at play. A seller wants to sell the emotional appeal of a big picture whereas purchasers are interested in trading small points of detail so as progressively, and little by little, to bring the price or reciprocal commitment down in size.

Depending on how important a deal may be to you, this will affect your emotional strength or weakness. The more important a result is to you, the less easy it is to negotiate. It is also important not to sell yourself short as this can also have the effect of the buyer believing that the purchase is less valuable than it really is. If the price is too low that reflects the value you put on yourself and your organization. If you believe your offer is really valuable, you will be confident to charge for that value.

Getting control

There is often a dilemma about who goes first in a negotiation but clearly you are in a better position if the other party goes first. You then have the opportunity to display an emotion rather than being on the receiving end of the other's reaction. Although you may be genuinely after a mutually acceptable result, you want it to be at the highest level you can achieve, and there is nothing wrong with that.

If you have to make concessions, you certainly do not have to give them away. If you trade such concessions then both parties can be satisfied.

When negotiating, it makes sense to reinforce your knowledge and confirm the extent of commitment by frequently clarifying the understanding between you. This is good for both you and the other party.

Never ask the boss

Finally, if you have the power to negotiate you have the power to decide; so it is not helpful to your case if you have to check back at base. This immediately weakens your potency as a negotiator.

Emotionally intelligent people like negotiating because it leads, or should lead to, win–win positions where the outcome is significantly better than an arbitrary and emotionally one-sided judgement. Also, you cannot negotiate effectively on a purely intellectual plane.

Appealing to investors

Most organizations, as they grow, will at some time be likely to seek outside financial investment whether from banks or other lenders, investment funds, other companies or wealthy individuals or groups. The process for doing so will vary according to circumstances but needs intelligence to be applied to secure the funding in the first place and to provide confidence that both the enterprise, and investors' funds, will be managed wisely.

Assuming that you've submitted a business plan to a potential investor in your company and your proposition is sufficiently attractive to be taken further, a critical test is your management team. Will the investor believe that his money is in safe hands? This then becomes a more emotional judgement.

Entrepreneurs come in all shapes and sizes

An entrepreneur's drive and compelling vision ensure new, exciting, wealth-creating ventures. But entrepreneurs are not perfect. If you lead from the front, someone's got to look after what's going on behind. The entrepreneur can only be truly effective if he or she is supported by people with management capabilities and is susceptible to their influence.

In a sense there is a management ecosystem where each member of a team contributes to and derives benefit from the complementary talents of his colleagues. Take one link away, however, and the system will lose its effectiveness.

A simple model for this (see Figure 8.2) can be represented as a management triad with an envisioner (or entrepreneur) at the apex, an enactor (or person who just gets things done) at one end of the base and an enabler (or person who helps convert ideas into substance) at the other.

FIGURE 8.2   Three qualities needed in a well-led and managed business

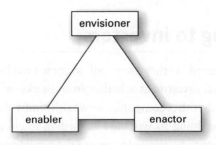

The envisioner, by nature, has dreams and big ideas, huge energy and a capacity for impatience, particularly with those who are slower

and do not necessarily buy in to all the visions. The envisioner is happy to work with someone who just likes doing things and 'enacts' the dream.

But the difficulty for the enactor is in filtering out the ideas that will work from the majority that probably will not. He doesn't always understand where the envisioner comes from, or know how to cope with the torrent of energy and constantly moving goalposts. Basically the two of them don't speak the same language, so this axis, although it can be productive, is frequently imperfect.

Imperfect axes

The envisioner, however, can communicate much more effectively with the enabler. Conversations more easily take place because of the enabler's social suppleness, any differences in view are more subtly managed and progress is more likely to be made.

The enabler, even without any visionary 'fuel' from the envisioner will be perfectly able to communicate with the enactor too. Where the enabler is an intermediary between the envisioner and the enactor, the system works; and vice versa.

The enabler provides filtration, an easy translation service, objectivity and process control to the enterprise. The other two can thus do what they do best without the constraints their limitations put upon them.

We can be blurred at the edges

Life's not quite that simple of course. It is more than likely that the principals in an organization have overlapping qualities. What the model does show, however, is that a blend of characteristics is needed to achieve the best management results for a business.

Investors will not necessarily look at these detailed points but they will want to ensure that visionary drive is supported by sustainable production or supply, well-directed marketing, rigorous sales activity and tight controls and that competency exists with every team member to deliver in these areas.

They may, of course, bring to bear complementary management talents of their own. That largely depends on the type of investor and their perception of any management gaps in the current team.

It's all about being a team

The emotionally intelligent entrepreneur and his team will be able to understand not just what an investor wants to hear in terms of credible numbers but also to have an insight into any likely reactions to the people involved in managing those funds credibly and productively.

The reasons people engage with investors in the first place are entirely to do with money and nothing to do with the investors' feelings. The money will be made available not just on the strength of the business case but also on factors such as confidence and belief. Emotional intelligence plays a critical role in putting feelings first and deferring the need for financial gratification until confidence has been established.

Many companies seeking investment – and there are many more seeking it than get it – expect that investors will be seduced into buying the idea. They don't realize that the idea is secondary to the confidence in the ability to deliver.

Chapter 09
Emotional intelligence and 20 business situations you could face

This section looks at different people, roles and departments in an organization and the choices they are likely to face in conducting their work. It looks at hypothetical situations they might encounter, the choices they face when seeking to achieve the best outcome, the factors that might influence their decision and what the outcomes could be. We cannot predict the outcomes, as every situation is completely individual, but we could make an educated guess given the nature of each decision postulated. The process can be summarized as a process that includes:

- Situations
- Choices
- Decisions
- Outcomes

The emotional intelligence aspects are to do with the quality of decisions as measured by the effectiveness of the outcomes achieved. Because situations are so specific to people and circumstances there are no right answers as such – it depends on who wants what. The optimum outcome for the person or people making the decisions could be benign and universally beneficial or it could serve selfish or partisan ends. The effectiveness of the result is in the eye of those who wanted it but may also be in the eye of those who didn't.

Having said that, in a business or organizational context, we are looking for outcomes designed primarily to deliver tangible benefits as widely and effectively as possible. So we will all be able to have a valid opinion about the relative merits of different decisions from a more altruistic standpoint.

The roles and departments illustrating the emotionally intelligent process are, as follows below, in Part A to do with business effectiveness and in Part B, personal effectiveness in a business context. The important question to ask yourself is what you would have done in similar circumstances and what you would have expected the outcomes to be.

PART A – BUSINESS EFFECTIVENESS

Human Resources departments in the selection, management and development of people

HR departments face an interesting challenge in recruitment insofar as they are usually trained in the selection process rather better than the managers who ultimately make the hiring decisions. However, they are likely to know rather less about the detailed requirements of the roles to be filled.

How *does*, for example, an HR person assess the capabilities of a cosmic physicist?

A frustration that can be encountered is that a hiring manager is impressed by what the HR person would see as being the wrong things, or oblivious to the right ones.

SITUATION 1
Influencing the choice of a sales candidate

A sales manager has shortlisted two possible candidates for a sales position. One of them is extrovert, confident and with easy charm. The other is quieter, serious and seems more hard-nosed. The manager, who strongly believes that 'people buy from people', is favourably influenced by the extrovert, particularly as he is a bit like himself.

The HR person, on the other hand, is thinking first and foremost about whom clients are more likely to trust and who will bring in more business in the long run. She wants the sales manager to choose but she also wants him not to make a decision that he will later come to regret. She does not really understand sales processes but knows whom, given the opportunity, she would more likely want to buy from. From her perspective the best outcome is what is best for the company and in her role, she has to make sure that the sales manager makes the best decision. The natural inclination might be to push for her preferred candidate but she needs to displace that feeling with what will be best for all.

Choices

- In her mind there are some different courses of action.
- She can leave the decision entirely up to the sales manager (because his judgement is probably better than hers and 'on his head be it' anyway).
- She can feel that the situation is unsatisfactory as it is and that it is her responsibility to do something about it – at the very least get a second opinion.
- She can say that she prefers the quieter candidate.
- She can seek solid evidence of both candidates' past performance and real-life achievements.

Decisions

She will want to take account of how the sales manager would react to each of the above. She needs also to consider how she will feel if she leaves it entirely up to him and what others in the organization might think if he chose unwisely. She also needs to take account of what it is that the organization really needs in terms of its goals and what impact the new appointee would have on its customers.

Outcomes

If she does nothing that is taking a, maybe unnecessary, risk for the business – which it is her job to avoid. So she is not doing her job properly and would find difficulty in influencing such decisions again.

If she asks for a second opinion, that's probably the right thing to do; provided there are agreed parameters for that opinion and the sales manager had been persuaded to support the idea.

If she states her preference, human nature being what it is, that could influence the decision the other way.

If she gains further evidence, that will help improve the quality of decision.

Conclusion

There are undoubtedly other choices available but the key to success is taking action. This must, however, be consistent with everyone's, not just your own, emotional harmony.

SITUATION 2
Blockages to managing and developing people

A shop-floor manager who has been with the company for 25 years has the reputation of being a bully. He is, however, useful to the organization in the sense that he does his job. He tends to tell people what to do because he thinks that is his role. He has difficulty with his staff who will do their job but go out of their way to avoid and frustrate him as much as possible.

When staff ask for things, such as time off, his instinct is to say no, simply because he has the power to do so. He also represents a career blockage to some bright young people in that he would only recommend for development and promotion if they had similar personal characteristics to him – because he thinks that is the best way to be.

Although a bully to his staff he is very ingratiating to those who are senior but does not enjoy their respect.

Two of his team have made an unofficial complaint to HR and are believed to be genuine. The natural inclination of the HR specialist might be either to dismiss the complaints or to assume they are right. But this should be displaced by a considered judgement that takes emotions and common sense into account.

Choices

- The HR specialist could take the company line, explain that production targets were being met and that, in those circumstances there was not a lot to be done.

- He could promise to have a word with the manager about improving his man-management skills on the basis that there were two anonymous complaints.

- He could decide to have a private word with others in the team in order to verify the situation.

- He could also seek feedback from other managers who will have observed whether his team in particular had particular issues.

- Having established the truth of the complaints he could produce a strategy for developing the manager's interpersonal and management skills.

- He could also look to have the manager displaced.

Decisions

The big question is whether an essentially ingrained set of attitudes and behaviours can be changed for the better and the difference it might make if they were. The status quo might be acceptable from a production point of view, but the company may be missing opportunities through developing talent that might otherwise make an even better contribution to the business.

Confronting the problem may be an explosive experience but the question is whether, in the longer run, it will improve business performance.

The HR specialist has to balance a set of conflicting needs but the business would not be well served in terms of its culture, management of change and well-being.

Conclusion

Once the subject has been broached – and it will have taken an emotional commitment to do so – it will be etched on the minds of the complainants and HR specialist. Doing nothing would be a less emotionally intelligent option since 'the hole in the dyke' has already been made and can only get larger. It is the management agility of the HR specialist that will be put most to the test in this circumstance.

Marketing specialists in their representations to customers and others

Every organization exists to satisfy a customer, whether it is a paying customer, clinical patient, taxpayer, member, user, voter, beneficiary and so on. We are primarily concerned in this section with customers who pay, as there is a specific and tangible link between what they pay and what they expect to get.

Successful marketing uses emotional intelligence (whether or not it is described as such) to create the optimum effect on potential customers. The innate desire is to tell people about our organization and our products, but this has to be tempered with an understanding that customers will want or be prepared to receive information, not just about those products and services but the value that they bring.

Before even considering marketing messages, however, it is critical to decide who will be the best people to receive them. Only then can you match message to potential customer. Although this is a truism, it is surprising how many people ignore it.

The AIDA principle is an important one here as it reflects the sequence in which people can be persuaded to respond and in effect manages their emotional journey. It would not be effective unless all the steps had been gone through in the order shown.

AIDA stands for Attention, Interest, Desire and Action as being the states you would progressively want to encourage. Behind these basics would be more subtle considerations such as confidence, trust, motivation and commitment, all of which are better managed with emotional intelligence.

Accountants in planning and in their handling of difficult financial challenges

Even with good accounting practices it is possible to sleepwalk into difficulty. Just small things can grow to become very significant unless addressed promptly.

In any organization there are conflicting pressures; those who want to spend money and those for whom the natural instinct is to reign back.

At a macro level, the worldwide recession that took hold in 2008 caused a great deal of debate about the extent of 'fiscal stimulus' (injection of taxpayers' and lenders' money) that would eventually solve the problem. The reality is that you can only be really wise after the event, but that does not stop the arguments about how bold or conservative to be in order to get the best outcome. There could be some interesting comparisons between the relative emotional intelligence of politicians and the recognized experts!

Because we all use it, everyone has an opinion about money, but skewed to reflect different 'views of the world'.

Service departments in their dealings with customers

When things are running smoothly then there are not usually many issues for service departments to resolve. It is when things go wrong for customers, or they feel poorly treated, that you are faced with choices and the decisions that need to be made. The relationship with customers is not only practical but involves a complex variety of emotions both for the service provider and those on the receiving end of that service. The satisfaction delivered by service functions is usually less exciting than the satisfaction gained through purchasing products. That is unless we are talking about services of the more personal kind such as in restaurants, for example.

Service that supports products is more often than not provided out of necessity rather than desire. The results of inadequate service very quickly translate into loss of reputation and income faster than good service builds it up.

SITUATION

The customer of a construction company has written to the customer care department of that company and this is a genuine extract from that letter:

> This is yet another example whereby XYZ Construction have been 'given an inch and taken a mile' and quite frankly this is not good enough but comes as no surprise.
>
> We can understand that [name supplied] is trying to appease everyone in this situation; however, her manner on the telephone was quite curt and has incensed us. ... we would therefore suggest that if you have no guarantee of completing the job by tomorrow afternoon that the [equipment] is removed and [then replaced] while we are away, and the job can be completed in the traditional fashion of slowly. An immediate response is expected.

Clearly these are very upset customers who have had, in their perception, a thoroughly unacceptable set of experiences. The likelihood of them buying from the same company again would seem remote.

The person on the receiving end of the letter will not be feeling great about it and possibly angry with someone – either the customer or her own colleagues whom she may feel have let the company down. But something clearly has to be done.

Choices

- There can be a formal response by letter that could apologize, explain or refute the complaint.

- An immediate telephone response could be considered as the best and quickest way of addressing the problem.

- The issue can be escalated to the firm's managing director so as to get him involved at that level.

- Immediate steps can be taken to provide the solution that the customer has asked for, explain what will be done and ensure it happens.

- Someone could be sent round immediately in order to 'face the music'.

Decisions

Because of the raw nature of emotions involved in the exchange, what has to be weighed up is the likely effect of each action on the customer and the consequent fortunes of the company. The decision would include having the right person involved in the issue's resolution, the timing and the action plan. If the customer is not appeased then many more people are going to be told about the company's failure in attitude and execution. The knock-on costs could be very expensive.

Clearly something has to be invested in order to achieve what in this case is likely to be the 'least worse' outcome.

The resolution is almost entirely about emotions and not practicalities. Some would suggest a big gesture (maybe a fully paid-for cruise?) as a low cost compared to the alternative bad publicity – and company members should probably not go along for the ride.

Outcomes

It will be difficult to resolve this situation to the satisfaction of the customer without promising some sort of recompense. The customer will not change his mind about what has happened. The only way is to move on with something sufficiently positive that it outweighs the problem. The construction company may want to consider paying an *ex gratia* sum of money, or suggesting something of value in kind. However, it may also consider that it is the customer's demands and unreasonableness that has caused a worse situation than was strictly necessary. The calculation is about how to do something proportionate without either party being further disadvantaged and annoyed. The customer's frame of mind can only be neutralized. It cannot reasonably be converted into happiness. The best outcome for the service department will be relief from the problem.

Conclusion

There are some situations where damage limitation is the only realistic option. The decision maker in this situation has to consider the odds of achieving that compared to risking a worse outcome. The emotional intelligence component is in judging the subtle difference between what will achieve the desired result and what will probably make the situation worse for both parties.

Sales departments in their approaches to acquiring and satisfying customers

It is often and mistakenly thought that selling is what you *do* to customers rather than being a mutually satisfactory transaction that leaves both parties pleased that they were able to do it. The trouble is that there is sometimes an unequal balance of power. Sometimes you are in a buyer's market and sometimes in a seller's market and each circumstance has an impact on the terms and conditions of the sale.

If you are selling commodity products then price will be very important. If you are selling luxury products or a package of solutions, price will be less important than the value that people place on the outcome.

The seller's organization is likely to be driven by financial targets so that the pressure to sell is high and can sometimes distort the need to ensure a good customer experience. There are some common scenarios that illustrate this.

SITUATION 1

A well-known charity is looking to increase the level of donations and legacies it attracts but has recently seen a decline due to others in the not-for-profit sector dramatically improving their fund-raising performance.

It is speaking to a number of marketing companies with a view to reinvigorating its fund-raising activities with their help.

As is commonly the case with such organizations, there is a formal process that they follow when selecting what in their terms is a strategically important medium- to long-term partner.

A number of meetings have been arranged. The first is to check the 'personal chemistry' between the charity's fund-raising team and the marketing company's personnel who would be chosen to work on the account. The second would be to review a set of strategic and creative proposals that demonstrate a sound understanding of the brief. They would also have to provide a convincing reason to be preferred. Two (of five) companies would then be shortlisted and invited to meet the directors for their assessment and feedback. Having consulted, the fund-raising team would then make its decision. The marketing company has to decide on its approach to winning the contract.

Choices

- It could take the fund-raising team out for a 'slap-up' meal at the end of the chemistry meeting.
- It could keep the chemistry meeting formal and businesslike to show how seriously it takes the account.

- As an opportunity has arisen to provide a charity speaker at an overseas conference, it could invite one of the directors to be that speaker and use that occasion to build a relationship.

- It could bring creative work to the chemistry meeting so as to pre-empt its rival marketing companies.

- It could second-guess what would be the best logical strategy for the charity with a view to 'ticking the boxes' and building on that during the process.

Decisions

The selection process having been dictated by the charity, the marketing company has to decide whether it will follow that to the letter and what the consequences would be of modifying it to maybe gain a slight competitive advantage.

In a competitive situation like this, received wisdom is that you should 'seek unfair advantage' otherwise you are unable to exert your full influence and could be inhibited from revealing your real capabilities by a highly subjective 'beauty parade'.

Arguably, in representing the charity to its public, your ability to achieve its competitive fund-raising aims through being creative about how you do it should be an appealing characteristic. Some might think it showed initiative while others might be sticklers for the rules. Gauging the personalities and emotional terms of reference of those likely to be involved in the meetings would be an essential piece of prior investigation.

Blatant 'emotional bribery' might work well with those with big egos but would be seen for what it was by those who were more detached and analytical.

Outcomes

The outcome is likely to be influenced more by trust than slick ideas. That trust is engendered through communication and so it would be really important to create opportunities for that communication, but not with superficial blandishments – it must be genuine.

The best outcome, given that there is a match between both organizations' values, is to enact a strategy that genuinely gets to know the target client and its people because that knowledge contributes to an easier mutual understanding and better likelihood of good teamwork.

As Margaret Thatcher famously said of Mikhail Gorbachev, 'I could work with that man', which is surely the biggest test.

Emotional intelligence plays an important role in understanding the personalities, attitudes and behaviours of the people with whom you would like to have a business partnership. You may consider that just going through the processes in a prescriptive way would lessen your ability to make a difference.

Conclusion

In winning business, companies often have to follow formal procedures that are there to ensure complete fairness of procurement. Although this is a laudable objective it can sometimes straitjacket companies who might otherwise be able to show with greater originality what they might be able to do.

Even when restrained by process, however, there is a lot that can be done to read in advance the likely emotional disposition of those who will (completely objectively?) make their selection of the suitable supplier.

Decision criteria are often said to depend on 'best value' as suppliers have often previously objected to organizations that always buy on price. The problem is that where price is quite specific, value is much more about perception. So there is no really good alternative to working out what would influence that perception and then doing something to make that happen.

SITUATION 2

A salesperson in a high-technology company has been falling short of his sales targets and has lost some confidence as a result. His view is that the main product on offer is not as competitive as others on the market. He also feels that he is being pressured by his manager who keeps asking questions about whether he has followed up specific leads, and he is then told what tasks he should do next.

A new regional sales director has been appointed and is questioning the performance of both the salesperson and his manager. He thinks that something should be done and is now taking up that challenge.

It may be the case that the salesperson is simply not competent enough and that the sales manager is right. It may also be the case that the sales manager is not up to his own role. Or it may be the case that neither of them is.

Choices

- He can suggest increasing the salesperson's targets as an incentive to better performance.

- He can suggest an action plan that requires a set number of speculative sales contacts to be made every week.

- He can arrange to 'shadow' the salesperson to find out whether there are things that could be done to increase his confidence and put him back on the road to success.

- He can check out what the sales manager thinks are ways in which his salesperson can gain more confidence and achieve better and more consistent results.

- He can interview and then fire the salesperson or his manager or both.

Decisions

All the above options, when dealing with an under-performing salesperson, are commonly practised despite the fact that some of them are more destructive than constructive. They may not, however, be good demonstrations of emotional intelligence.

Increasing targets, when not related to the reality of the situation would not sit well with him emotionally.

Prescribing set numbers of sales contacts per week might work in situations where what is being sold is a commodity. It would be less likely to work in a more complex sales environment where the quality of calls rather than the volume has proved to be more important and effective.

Effectiveness in a sales role calls for motivation, energy and resilience, so these are the qualities that should a) be tested and b) encouraged. In other words it is better to address the person more than the process.

Then there is the question of whether to take ownership or encourage it to remain with the sales manager, or whether to approach the challenge as a team.

Outcomes

The likely outcome of increasing pressure will be increased stress – which is not what is necessarily wanted when looking for improvement. Looking for solutions is likely to be more effective in that it neutralizes the boss/subordinate aspects of the transaction and allows participation in the co-operative process of achieving the result.

History and previous experience will have a bearing on the effectiveness of outcome and should have been factored into the process.

Given that the salesperson was in all other respects a reasonably competent person, it is likely that the consultative approach to his 'rehabilitation' would be the most effective way to proceed.

Also to be considered is the emotional outcome on others in the business from a draconian as compared with a balanced and fair approach.

The optimum outcome is better salesperson, better sales manager, better results and greater satisfaction all round. A less satisfactory outcome is if people have to be replaced and there are new people, new costs and knock-on effects to be managed. The decision has a lot hanging on it.

Conclusion

The situation described is not an uncommon one and there is a tendency in sales environments, where directness and extroversion are common personality traits, to take decisions that reflect the emotional orientation of those involved. This may not always be in the best long-term interest of the people or the organization, so there is great benefit in emotionally intelligent reflection that substitutes impulsive reactions with those whose consequences have been more fully considered.

Production departments in their handling of labour and assets

Despite the enlightenment of today's society, there can often be a divide between management priorities and workers' attitudes. This can be particularly apparent when there is a contrast in lifestyles. Big cars in specially nominated parking spaces, for example, contrast starkly with the often older and more modest transport of the majority.

The perceived divide may still be between owner and workers or it may be between those managers who, for example, have engineering degrees that differentiate them from those who have no formal qualifications to give them status. That is why many workers consider that they just have a 'nine-to-five' job and feel little emotional attachment to the firm.

Factories and workshops tend not to be places where people are cosseted and those who work in such an environment will often differentiate themselves from the more effete 'pen-pushers' who work in offices. It need not be like this but the company has to deliberately try to align people with the aims of the business and see their different roles as contributing to common and mutually beneficial ends. In other words, to be a worthwhile way of spending a third of your life, the job has to have a higher purpose than just paying the bills.

SITUATION

A manufacturing company with a headcount of around 50 provides high-quality fittings both to commercial and domestic building contractors and, through distributors, to the home improvement market. The company is run by its owner and also employs a small but experienced team of technically proficient managers. There are three foremen on the shop floor and the company manages its own transport.

Staff at this company can sometimes be slapdash and so are the foremen in their casual policing of production standards. This results in a disproportionate level of faulty goods being returned, but being in the right market with the right goods means that the company is still relatively successful in retaining its market share. There is an incentive scheme for 100 per cent attendance every month but people seem to prefer taking their 'sickies' to earning the extra money.

The owner drives an expensive Jaguar and has just bought a helicopter.

The company has just appointed a new general manager with the remit of improving business performance and, in particular, profit. He also wants to change the culture so that the company is a better and brighter place to work. There is a choice of things he has considered that he might do.

Choices

- Develop a competitive team structure where groups of individuals are given tangible rewards – retail shopping tokens or tickets to special events, for example – as a result of top team performance.

- Brand these teams with the names of high-performing racing teams and provide posters to support that.

- Retrain or replace the current foremen depending on the commitment to a new set of goals.

- Put up a series of notices to remind staff of the importance of sticking to standards and hold company meetings, in the firm's time, to provide briefings and updates.

- Nominate or find a factory leader who embodies the right personal characteristics to galvanize the organization into consistently positive behaviour.

- Bring in Quality Assurance consultants to work in co-operation with existing managers to introduce new standards that everyone, because they have been involved, will support.

Decisions

Depending on the professional quality of the consultants involved and the willingness of management to pursue specific, measurable and achievable goals, it often works to engage outside help.

This would not necessarily be as good as a permanent member of staff acting as a permanently present 'leader' that others could be motivated to follow, but maybe a hybrid solution would be useful.

Clearly there has to be some intervention with the foremen in the business as they are not fulfilling their leadership roles in its best interests. The expression comes to mind, 'If you can't change the people, change the people!' as they are a critical link to future success and can make or break a change process.

Different motivational devices can be tried but they are no substitute for changing the whole culture for the better. They are more effective in support of something than in changing attitudes.

Outcomes

As things currently stand, the sole purpose of many workers in the factory is to earn a day's pay rather than help the business achieve a known and shared goal. They may be involved but are not committed – and neither are the foremen.

Exhortations to improvement are not likely to work as people feel detached from the owner's purpose, which to them seems to be around lifestyle and wealth.

From the owner to the most junior employee, there needs to be a common and emotionally uplifting purpose to which everyone will willingly commit. Once that is understood and shared, the work can begin on the structures, systems and processes to make it happen.

Whether this is the prerogative of the owner or he can delegate the responsibility to someone who is competent to take up the challenge, could be a matter for debate. The company is not 'broken' in any sense and does not need to be 'fixed' but the status quo is less than satisfactory than it need be for everyone involved across the firm. In this regard, doing nothing is not an option.

Conclusion

The above scenario is not uncommon and results from a business having grown but not adapted to the changing circumstances that growth brings. What works in one stage of a company's development does not necessarily work well in another. Often, the owner's 'ability to do' is what makes the company successful but as it grows becomes a less critical factor. Knowing when to delegate responsibility and 'let go' is difficult for many owners but ultimately restricts the effectiveness of the organization.

This is not overtly a factor in the above situation but probably underlies the problems that have emerged.

Company owners in their business decisions and leadership roles

As referred to in the situation outlined above, owning a business that has the potential to expand means the possibility of managing it through several stages of growth. The word 'entrepreneur', however, does not necessarily denote someone whose abiding passion is to make money in as large quantities as possible and is a label that can be misleading. Motives for starting a business can be many and various, just as there are many different ways of running it. When people start up businesses these boil down into broadly four ways of categorizing their intentions but, of course, there are many more ramifications from each one of those. Table 9.1 shows those four basic intentions.

TABLE 9.1 Personal motivators for starting and running a business

Create	**Invest**
Manage	**Govern**

Inventors are essentially creative people who want to do what no one has done before. Investors are mainly looking for capital growth and are preoccupied with how best to achieve it. Managers love the buzz they get from running smooth and efficient operations and nurturing growth through other people and other resources. Those whose preferred style is to govern are concerned with governance procedures, position and control. There often comes a point for the company owner when he or she has to decide to continue with a leadership role or delegate to someone else – maybe someone in the family or someone from outside.

SITUATION

The owner of a successful knowledge-business company employing 35 staff was increasingly involved in activities not directly associated with the business and was enjoying them. He started the company in order to make a mark and had the support of a business partner with whom he shared the management burden. The partner retired and that left him to manage the business on his own. It became apparent that what he thought was his appetite for running a business was becoming less interesting than other things that he was now doing. He therefore decided to hire an external manager, but not having done so before was not sure what credentials to look for in someone who could competently take over.

Choices

- He interviewed someone with an accountancy background who had been recommended for the position as being perceptive, disciplined and reliable – if a little boring.

- He ran into an old friend who had been a senior manager in a large corporation and was looking for new challenges – but had never run a business nor worked in one with only 35 staff.

- A headhunter had recommended someone from the same industry who had held senior positions in it but not been put fully in charge of any business.

- He personally admired the sales director of a competitor and wondered if he would not be the right choice because of his industry connections.

- He had been offered the services of an experienced managing director whose previous company had folded. As he was coming up to retirement age, this person would be an interim as compared to permanent appointment.

Decisions

The accountant was the antithesis of the owner in that he was relatively introverted, risk averse and interested in detail. The company would be safe in his hands but would not be inspirationally led.

The old 'corporate' friend was clearly a competent manager but there was no clue as to his likely performance when leading a business and developing its growth strategy.

The headhunter's nomination might be good at 'the business of the business' but could he run the 'business', having never run one before?

The competitor's sales director could be good in developing business but would he be equipped with the financial knowledge, operational know-how and governance disciplines that the role demanded?

The 'soon-to-retire' ex managing director would cover all the bases but would he be motivated and driven to succeed as much as would a younger candidate?

Outcomes

The choice revolves around what the owner still wants the business to become. If he wants it to be a source of steady future income then the accountant might do.

If he wants to put friendship and personal trust over experience, he could rely on the commitment but would be unsure about a good outcome.

If he went with the headhunter's choice, apart from paying a big fee for the appointment, he would also be taking a bigger risk through relying on his judgement.

The sales director would be a risk and other aspects of the business than sales might eventually fall apart.

The safe ex managing director would do for the moment but would not provide a lasting solution and would create the need to go through the exercise again in a couple of years – risking the owner being dragged back into the business during the intervening period.

Conclusion

An important factor missing from the above is the relationship between the owner and an incumbent managing director. The owner cannot completely abdicate responsibility for the business and has to ensure that the person he appoints is fully accountable to him. That is not an interfering role but a wise status check and counselling opportunity. The appointment will not work unless very clear terms of reference have been given, performance expectations spelled out and agreement reached about what will happen if that performance does not live up to expectations.

There is a high failure rate when owners appoint new managing directors to take over their management roles. This is mostly because the vetting is insufficiently rigorous in the first place and clear terms of reference have not been established. This leads to strain in the relationship and an eventual parting of the ways, mostly because of personality differences that then become exaggerated.

The emotionally intelligent way to appoint a new person to take over is to clearly articulate the outcomes required and appoint only against a solid commitment and clear delivery strategy that has been meticulously prepared.

Managers in handling people, activities, resources and communication

If you were to ask what a manager actually does to further the work of his organization, it can broadly be limited to just four things – management of activities, management of people, management of resources and management of communication. Quite often it is the failure to manage communication that negates the effectiveness of an otherwise competent manager, but there are other situations as well.

SITUATION

You believe that you are a relatively competent manager with sincere values and intentions. You also know that you have some weaknesses and that if you were to address some of them you could become appreciably more effective.

Despite your best endeavours, things do not always go as you want them to go, your staff members do not always respond in the way that you would like them to and projects are sometimes over time and over budget.

Those above you are supportive but have probably 'pigeon-holed' you as being as good as you can get.

Choices

- There are various things that you think you should work on but have to decide where you should start. They include the following.
- Managing your own time better.
- Studying to understand principles of leadership and management.
- Setting clearer objectives for you and your team.
- Working on a more positive management style.

- Setting a policy and process for better communication – and sticking to it.
- Developing a better understanding of team-building skills.
- Developing your own people more effectively.
- Having a better focus on delivery, client satisfaction and profit.

Decisions

The first decision is whether to focus on your own development or that of your staff as the higher priority. Would you be able to focus on staff development without first receiving training to put some parameters in place?

Would the multiplier effect of developing staff be greater than the single effect of developing you? What would be the short- as compared to long-term gains?

The word 'communication' is about *sharing* information. Should you communicate your intentions and personal objectives to staff in order to enlist their support for a more general improvement and would this show you as being a more positive and proactive operator or not?

Should you formally put a better system of communication in first?

Or, bearing in mind the manifold benefits of teamwork, would you do something about team building as a main priority?

Or should you first of all seek an outside assessment of myself and arrange coaching input as to an improvement strategy you could adopt?

Outcomes

Unless you have some measure of where you are genuinely good and where you could improve, you will depend solely on my own judgement to create and implement an improvement plan. This would not be as quick or as objective as external input.

One of the big issues is where you may be a blockage and if you don't know at present then that in itself is a blockage to progress. It may also be that 360-degree assessment would help and also encourage staff to believe that things will improve and that they can contribute to that improvement.

Then there is the question of delegation and whether you should rely on others more to take on responsibilities that mitigate my weaknesses.

Also, what would the impact of improvement look like? If we do not set goals and milestones it will be difficult for us to know.

However, the biggest impact might be just in the fact that you are actively seeking to improve – a positive step in the right direction.

Conclusion

Many managers are oblivious to their shortcomings so it shows a degree of emotional intelligence to admit to them and do something about ensuring better things for all in the future. Because 'no man is an island' your staff members are inextricably involved with you anyway – for better or for worse. It therefore makes intellectual as well as emotional sense to involve them. It is not a natural reaction to involve others, as most of us would prefer to keep our bad points a secret – so it is emotionally more difficult but wiser to do so. There is a wide range of choices about what can be done but external input, although it might cost something, would no doubt help the organization achieve better outcomes faster. The decisions themselves would depend on that feedback.

The unenviable task of selecting people for redundancy

SITUATION

A manager has been asked to trim his department by three members of staff, to enable the company to be more competitive and meet its financial targets. There are no clear contenders and no one has applied for voluntary redundancy. It is crucial that he can justify the method he uses for selecting the unfortunate staff members. Above all he must avoid showing any bias towards a particular member of staff. An unemotional approach is called for which requires (paradoxically) a high degree of emotional intelligence.

Selecting people for redundancy is a difficult and often painful task, for legal and personal reasons. The overriding aim is for fairness and the process involves balancing all the factors that can legitimately be taken into account when laying people off. The manager will need to be aware of what constitutes reasonable grounds. In most cases he will have been advised by the HR department if this is not something he already knows. In attempting to make the best decision, the natural inclination might be to go for the most obvious candidates. But the selection procedure should not be taken forward by the easiest route. Every aspect and each person will need to be thoroughly considered and carefully balanced against the others, so that the right choices are made. This should ensure a result that is best for all concerned: the individual members of staff, the department going forward with reduced numbers and the company as a whole.

Choices

- In the mind of the manager are the following different courses of action.

- He can decide on who should leave by virtue of length of service. If this factor is being taken into account it could be used as the only benchmark – ie 'last in, first out'.

- He could take a financial assessment since redundancies are often driven by monetary constraints. Here he could argue that the most expensive personnel should leave.

- On the issue of skills, he could make someone redundant because their particular skill set is no longer required, or the member of staff does not possess the relevant skills for the job they are doing.

- There is another aspect – performance – that he could consider. This one can be difficult, as it requires evidence to prove that someone's performance is below the acceptable level.

- Behaviour, absences, discipline are other reasons the manager could cite. The company would have documentation to show which staff have poor attendance records or have been disciplined for inappropriate attitude or behaviour.

- Another factor the manager should consider is company loyalty. If some members of staff are less supportive of company ethos and culture than others, this could put them in the frame for possible redundancy.

Decisions

The manager has some difficult decisions to make.

If he takes the view 'last in, first out', he might be dispensing with a bright young, keen employee who could be of great value to the company in future. Perhaps this member of staff has not been in post long enough to fully show his potential.

If he works on the line of the most highly paid members of staff should be the ones to leave the company, it could be detrimental to the department as a whole. Highly paid staff usually represent a net worth to the company otherwise they wouldn't have reached their particular level of salary scale. Should the manager decide to let them go the company could lose much relevant knowledge and expertise.

On the issue of skills, the manager cannot make a member of staff redundant just because they can't do something. The person may not be able to touch-type, for example, but for this to be a factor for possible redundancy, part of their job skill set has to include the ability to type at speed. If the skills don't impinge in any way, this does not constitute grounds for redundancy.

If the manager is looking at staff performance, he must be able to show clearly with sufficient documentary evidence that a person's performance is poor despite having been given the opportunities for on-the-job training, mentoring and support from good line-management. Without this it would be difficult to prove grounds for redundancy. Every employer's nightmare is the prospect of defending an 'unfair dismissal' claim in court.

Should a member of staff have a poor attendance record, it is essential that the reasons for their absences from work are carefully investigated. Should it be because of the ill health of a dependent partner, child or elderly parent these absences could be deemed unavoidable. Whereas someone with no family or caring commitments whose pattern it is to 'pull a sickie' on a regular basis due to overindulgence of one sort or another is a different case entirely.

The loyalty factor is a worthy consideration. If the manager is aware of troublemakers among his staff who incite others to disloyal behaviour (strike/working to rule), this could be justification for selecting someone for redundancy.

Outcomes

The emotionally intelligent manager has to think carefully about who he makes redundant and the effect it has on the people themselves. He cannot simply make 'heads roll' so as to tick the required boxes. He must consider the outcomes from various angles.

The company has to meet its required redundancy targets. He can't just say that there isn't anyone suitable so none of his staff is leaving at present. Also it is the manager's responsibility to ensure that his department is able to function satisfactorily once the selected candidates have left.

He has to choose people who will not prevent the department from being operationally effective. If, after he's made his selection, none of the remaining staff know how to use computerized customer accounts records to input and retrieve orders and sales information correctly, the department will soon grind to a halt.

He could consider offering two people a job-share or asking if someone would be prepared to work three days a week rather than five. This might enable him to reduce the number of redundancies from three to one. Perhaps one or other of the highly paid members of staff could be persuaded to take a salary cut?

But what about the people who are to be made redundant, how will they survive if left without a job for a while? Someone might be struggling to pay a mortgage, with the prospect of facing repossession and being homeless as a worst-case scenario if they do not find alternative employment quickly.

Some candidates, if made redundant, may not have a problem in relocating should they find new employment. However, an employee with a family would find the prospect of looking for new work far more difficult. A partner's job could be in the balance, as well as new schools for their children; for them redundancy is a far bigger issue than someone without such constraints.

The best way forward is for the manager to keep his staff informed, with as much notice as possible about planned redundancies.

Should final decisions have to be taken – say within three months – he could invite his staff to talk to him if they have particular fears. If he shows sympathy and awareness of how it may affect them, he is likely to be supported by those staff who remain after the redundancies have been made.

The more alert he is to his staff's personal circumstances the more this will help him improve the quality of his decision.

Conclusion

The emotionally intelligent manager will have to balance all these factors, while still taking the necessary action. His decision however should be compassionate (in relation to the human capital) yet unemotional, so that from the points of view of the department's ongoing effectiveness and the financial viability of the organization he has made the best possible decision. The win–win situation is to select the right people for redundancy, without inflicting unnecessary pain, while retaining the respect and loyalty of the remaining members of staff.

How to deal with an impossible boss

SITUATION

An employee finds his boss impossible to work for, yet his colleagues do not. Is this his fault? Is this the boss's fault, or a bit of each? How should the employee apply emotional intelligence to remedy a situation where it is far easier to be subjective than objective?

The employee must examine what he finds intolerable about the situation. For example: is the boss really 'not his type'? Is it his boss's working style that is at variance to his own? Is it a personality clash? It is important to identify what he thinks is the source of the problem between them. If the boss behaves well towards other colleagues but is totally unreasonable to him, he must discover (by looking inwards or outwards) why he's singled out for such treatment. There has to be a reason for the way the boss treats him, if it is not something the rest of the staff have to put up with.

He should take stock of the situation from a personal perspective. The employee should, at the earliest opportunity, analyse his own behaviour, emotions, attitudes and values. He should go through a self-awareness checklist. Is he, for example, a difficult person? Has a similar situation ever arisen before in his previous work experience? If so, he could reflect on this to see whether something he did in the past could help him now in his present position.

Another step would involve the employee talking to his colleagues. Requesting their help in exploring the reasons for the boss's unreasonable behaviour towards him would shed more light on the situation. Perhaps the colleagues aren't aware of it happening. Once they have been alerted to the problem, they may recall occasions where the boss behaved in a similar way towards them. If this is the case, the employee should find out what they did to ameliorate the situation. Having made them aware of the situation, his colleagues may back him up when they see instances of the boss's unpleasant treatment of the employee. This would be an effective deterrent for the boss should other members of staff rally to the defence of the victim.

If it is a personality issue, is it possible that it could be jealousy on the part of the boss? For some reason does this employee pose a threat to him? Is the person particularly competent in an area in which the boss does not excel? Could the boss fear that the employee is waiting to step into his shoes? In which case being around this employee could emphasize his insecurity. He may even take the view that 'attack' is the best form of 'defence' of his position in the company. The best way of dealing with this issue is for the harassed employee to instigate a one-to-one discussion with the troublesome boss.

If none of the above helps, the employee could ask to see his boss's boss or make a complaint about his boss's behaviour to the HR department. This step should be taken as a last resort, if the employee feels he has exhausted alternative avenues of approach.

Choices

- Some people leave their jobs (even when they like what they do) because they aren't happy working for someone they don't get on with. This is an option and should be kept firmly in mind by the employee when considering other actions he could take.

- Alternatively, the employee could consider staying put in his present position if any of the following are likely to occur within a short time: he is going to be promoted or transferred to another office or department; his boss is looking for another job or coming up for retirement.

- The employee could try a more subtle approach, such as minimizing contact with his boss. This is obviously dependent to a certain extent on the sort of work he does. If appropriate he could begin by asking permission to work from home a couple of days a week, or put himself beyond the reach of the boss by asking if he could undertake more business travelling.

- The direct and perhaps quickest action he could take is to approach the boss personally, by asking him (to his face) why he is on the receiving end of such treatment. This should be done using an assertive rather than an aggressive style. The employee should ask the boss to cite specific causes, and say he is anxious to do whatever he can to resolve things between them if he can possibly do so. If he is a bully, the boss may well bluster about there being nothing specific or wrong, but he might back off from such behaviour in future.

- There is an option for the employee to show the boss, by example, that he is not going to allow the boss's unreasonable behaviour to affect him. The employee could volunteer for tasks that might take the boss by surprise. For example, if it is difficult for the employee to work late sometimes because of family commitments and the boss always points this out in a disparaging way, he could offer to come in to work on a weekend if that will help. Anything that would undermine the boss's unjustified complaints about his work methods would be effective.

- Making a complaint about the boss to the HR department or the boss's direct boss requires serious consideration. This is a process that once started cannot be undone. The employee must first be sure in his own mind that this course of action would not in fact make the situation worse. Could he be certain of getting a sympathetic hearing? What he decides to do depends to a large extent on the type of organization he works for, the company culture and if similar procedures have ever been successfully instigated in the past by other employees.

Decisions

This harassed employee has to weigh up some tricky issues, but by applying emotional intelligence and some careful thought, he has a number of routes to improve the situation.

He could simply decide to 'stick with it' and maintain the status quo for the time being. This should not be regarded as a passive stance. A waiting game requires a degree of fortitude and sometimes can prove a strong tactical move in such a strategy. The important thing is for the employee to have a set time limit. He must promise himself that should the situation not have improved or changed (and certainly if it has worsened) in three months, then he gives himself permission to hand in his notice at that time.

Discussing the matter with his boss to air the issues between them is a viable option. With a reasonable person, this action can have a good effect on all parties – the employee, the boss and the department as a whole. But depending on the boss's character it may or may not work. The boss may be deaf to all entreaties and reasonable behaviour may not be his strong point.

The employee could ask colleagues to act as witnesses on his behalf with regard to the boss's treatment of him. They may be prepared to support their colleague informally, but would they stand up against this manager (as he is also their own direct superior) in a formal context, perhaps putting their own situations at risk in the process?

Should the boss's behaviour have become intolerable, making a formal complaint about him may be the best correct course of action for the unfortunate employee. This would require the HR department investigating whether there are disciplinary issues involved. The unreasonable boss would have to be interviewed by them, which could escalate things fairly swiftly.

Outcomes

The key question for the employee to answer is: how much does the job mean to him? This is where the application of emotional intelligence comes in: being detached from a painful personal situation, considering the situation from all angles and making an unemotional choice. Depending on his answer – and it must be seriously considered and totally honest – the most appropriate action will become clear to him.

For example, if the job is unusual, and the employee is unlikely to get other work similar to it or as personally satisfying elsewhere, he may have little choice if he wishes to keep working but to stay put. The best option then is to try to make the subtle adjustments to his working routine so that his boss's behaviour is more tolerable.

If, on the other hand, he could get a similar job (at the same level, comparable satisfaction levels, salary scale, geographical location) that would eliminate at a stroke all the unpleasantness associated with his current work, why wait? He should start looking for new employment immediately. He has nothing to lose and much to gain.

Conclusion

The decision whether to quit his job or stick with it, rests with the employee and him alone. Once he's explored the various options – checking that it's not his fault; asking advice and support from his colleagues; talking directly to his boss about how to improve their working relationship; appealing to the HR department or his boss's boss for help; he has covered the bases.

Whatever action he decides to take, the employee must make sure that it has a positive effect on his well-being, improves the situation immediately, and enables him to go to work each day in a cheerful state of mind.

A young executive finds his new promotion causes more pain than pleasure

SITUATION

When he was told he had been promoted, the young executive thought his working life would be perfect. A more senior position in a company in which he thrived with responsibilities and challenges that he was eager to shoulder, were about to be his. Perhaps he had hoped for advancement and actively looked forward to such a thing happening. How come then, within a few short weeks of taking up his new role, he was beginning to wish that it had never happened to him? What was wrong? Why has this enhanced status of his turned sour so quickly and become both awkward and difficult? Why were previously pleasant colleagues behaving in a disgruntled fashion?

There are a number of possible contributing factors, all of which should be considered, when working out how to deal with such a situation. Emotional intelligence requires an all-encompassing view of a problem; ascertaining the choices available; balancing the actions a person can take against the outcomes they may achieve in the process.

Perhaps the young executive, in this scenario, had been promoted above former colleagues? Or he had gained preferment over people who were older in years (but not more senior in status) than he? One person in particular showed resentment about his new position. Why did this encourage more departmental colleagues to show an openly hostile attitude towards him? He was now in a supervisory role over them, yet this fact caused upset and distress across the department.

Dealing with the effects of promotion can be a difficult situation for anyone – not only those who achieve it rapidly but also those who don't. In the young executive's case it was a well-deserved preferment, as he had been an obvious candidate. He was well suited to his new status yet any new role takes time to settle into. The 'honeymoon' period in this instance has been so brief as to be almost non-existent. It was obvious a number of his staff had issues with the new status quo.

The young executive knew that some members of his staff would require tactful handling. He was anxious not to alienate them by exerting his authority unduly in the first few days. Yet would he risk losing the respect of his staff in his new position if he was perceived as inactive? What was the best course of action to make it clear that he was now 'in charge'? And was there anything he could do to win over his staff and earn respect as their new boss?

Choices

- Applying emotional intelligence in this scenario, the courses of action available to the newly promoted young executive could include the following.

- Ensure that he maintains a high level of self-confidence. He must find a way to keep his motivation positive, because there is nothing more demoralizing than trying to work with staff who are unsupportive.

- Would doing nothing for the time being, leaving the staff to carry on, be the better way? He might be hoping that things will settle down in time. Remember that suspending judgement and not reacting emotionally requires courage. On the other hand problems that are left unresolved rarely go away.

- Because the new boss was so recently one of their peers, the staff show signs of slack behaviour and performance. The young man wants to stop this promptly and firmly without making the atmosphere in the department worse.

- Should he do something to stamp his authority on his staff? He wants to earn their respect and trust but how?

- As he is facing personal resentment from one particular colleague, he must at the first opportunity find out why this person is so upset.

Decisions

The young manager has a number of options available to him.

The first problem to address is the matter of his self-confidence. With everyone around him grumbling, and feeling dissatisfied, the young executive should remember why he was promoted. Other people (more senior than he) felt he had the ability to manage staff and cope with increased responsibility. If they have confidence in him, he should have confidence in himself and not allow doubts to creep in.

Improving the atmosphere in the department could be done by keeping calm and making few if any changes. This would give the staff time to settle down of their own accord. He could, for example, make a conscious decision not to change anything unless it really needed to be done. The staff would see that he was not making change for change's sake. The risk here is that he is doing nothing to earn their respect.

However, if he does intend to make his mark, he could instigate some new procedures to start the process of unification. Setting up a one-hour staff meeting to establish workload priorities first thing on a Monday morning would be one way of drawing the department together. Or a more informal 'happy hour' on a Thursday evening after work, if he wanted to set a more relaxed style of management.

Because he is a lot younger than some of his staff, they do not find it easy to respect him. It is up to the young executive to prove to his older staff that he is the exception; he may be younger in years but that doesn't mean he can't be a good boss. He could call a meeting of all the staff to examine the issues and ask for their support and suggestions for creating the best possible working atmosphere.

The member of staff who seemed to be particularly hostile to the young executive should be interviewed as a matter of urgency. If it transpires that this person had (for whatever reason) regarded himself as the rightful occupant of the position now seemingly snatched from his grasp, there is something that can be done. The young manager can show sympathy for him and explain that he should not be negative and feel he has 'lost out'. He can directly request the support and advice of his former colleague, in this way he may gain an ally and silence his critical views.

Outcomes

The young executive wanted to win on all counts.

He needed to keep himself focused and clear about how he was going to make his new role a success, be a good manager to his staff and an example of departmental excellence to the company. So he took pains to keep his own motivation at a high level.

He changed the way the department operated yet allowed some breathing space so that the staff didn't feel he was constantly 'on their backs'. Time is a healer and he was patient with the staff who needed to adjust to the new situation.

He made sure that although he was no longer at the same level as his staff, he maintained a friendly approach towards them. The informal social event each week improved the atmosphere across the department.

The person who was particularly annoyed at having 'lost out' to the new manager agreed to give him the benefit of his experience. This way the manager won over the resentful colleague and made him feel important and of use. The new manager had put himself in the other person's place and thought about how he would like to be treated if the situations had been reversed.

Conclusion

The newly promoted manager proved that he was capable of handling all the complexities of people management. He thought about the issues facing him from his own, his staff and his former colleague's point of view. By taking a 360-degree assessment of the situation he was able to restrain himself from knee-jerk reactions. He made a number of emotionally intelligent decisions that created a healthier working environment in his department; this benefited not only himself but also his staff and the company.

An employee has too much work and not enough time

SITUATION

The administrator holds an important position in her department. Everyone depends on her to process work quickly, otherwise information management slows up and backlogs occur. The problem is that however fast she works, the quicker urgent jobs appear on her desk. The more she does, the more there is to do. She is reluctant to start working late, or arrive earlier each morning. This could quickly be taken as 'the norm' and her colleagues would take advantage of the fact that she is doing longer hours every day of the working week.

The administrator is married with a family. The last thing she wants is to encroach on her personal/family time. It is a never-ending cycle of having too much to do and not enough time in which to do it. All this stress is beginning to make her unwell. Unless she can control the situation, her health will deteriorate. If she takes sick leave and is absent from work, the greater the backlog when she returns to her desk. She is getting desperate and fears that it will finally reach the stage where she will have no choice but to leave the job and company that she loves.

Choices

- Taking action is essential: there is no likelihood of the situation improving if left unchecked. The administrator must be proactive. What are her options?

- First, a meeting with her boss to explain the problems she faces at work. This should include a description of the unhealthy symptoms the work situation is producing as well as a number of proposals for solving these issues.

- The administrator could request training in time management and delegation skills.

- She could enquire about any flexibility in her work pattern so that she can manage her workload better without encroaching on her family/personal life.

- She might ask if there are any plans to increase the size of the department; would the creation of a part-time assistant's post be a possible solution?

- The possible relocation of her work desk to a place where there are less interruptions might be another possibility. If somewhere could be found where her colleagues can't dump things on her desk in passing, it would put her out of reach of their constant demands.

- She could take steps to eliminate the build up of stress by doing something like yoga, squash or swimming outside working hours. These might improve her health and her attitude of mind.

- She could ask her doctor to give her a sick note and sign her off for a few weeks while she takes time to decide her future.

Decisions

Applying emotional intelligence, the administrator has thought what the ideal solution for her would be. She enjoys her work, her salary helps support the family. She feels that with certain adjustments in the workplace she could cope better and work more effectively.

The administrator has decided that being proactive is the way forward. If she is assertive (not passive, not aggressive) her boss should give her a fair hearing. She prepares for her meeting with the boss with possible solutions, not bringing him just the problem.

The question of whether the job comes before her family or health is already decided. Nothing is more important than her family and their well-being but carrying on as she is, and becoming ill, is not an option.

But a change of work pattern could help. If her boss were to agree to her having some help from an assistant, or she was allowed to delegate certain tasks to, say, the IT department, this would be a solution to the overwork and stress. She could ask her boss whether instead of accepting her annual salary increase she could have some extra days' holiday instead.

The option of relocating her workstation could solve the problem of colleagues interrupting the administrator. Such a small adjustment would break the habit that has developed of the administrator being accessible from all sides. People would not walk past her desk; this could reduce the amount of work she is given.

Time-management courses or delegation-skills training would be a sensible solution. In-house training may be available and this could improve the administrator's output and personal effectiveness. It would increase her self-confidence if she feels she is able to handle stressful situations correctly. She would then be less likely to be overwhelmed by her workload in future.

Taking up a relaxing outside activity would be something the administrator could arrange for herself. She could benefit from the regular exercise, it would make her fitter and less prone to illness caused from work-related stress. She could even combine it with family activities at a local health club or sports centre.

Outcomes

Whichever of the proposals she has put to her boss is accepted, the administrator will find an improvement in her work situation and a more positive mental attitude generally.

Each suggestion can be quickly implemented and none of them is going to cost the company huge amounts of money. Most of them are positive suggestions and will increase her efficiency and raise her motivation.

The possible solutions she can implement herself, including relaxation, sport or exercise, are not difficult to arrange. Organizing her priorities better will reduce her stress levels and decrease her chances of being ill.

Conclusion

The administrator was able to put forward a number of options. She knew the problem had a solution, it was just a matter of finding what combination of change would work best. The emotionally intelligent approach was to give her manager time to consider which changes would be best to put into practice. He was offered flexibility and freedom of choice by her suggestions. A mutually acceptable compromise was achieved. This reduced the stressful workplace situation and the administrator's attitude and output improved. There were no far-reaching changes but small adjustment for her and her family to adjust to. The result was an improved work/life balance and a healthier attitude.

A customer services assistant has to deal with an angry customer

SITUATION

An experienced customer services assistant found himself on the receiving end of an angry tirade. Something had gone wrong with a major order. The customer was furious with the company, its service and its staff and wanted satisfaction. The customer assistant needed to take action and reduce the potentially damaging situation that was unfolding before him. Deciding on the courses of action available to him require the application of intelligence, sympathy and practicality.

In customer services, when something goes wrong, the best advice is to find out what the problem is quickly, then seek to remedy the grievance in the customer's interests. There is nothing more awkward than a customer getting angrier and angrier, whether it is down the phone, in the middle of the reception area, by e-mail or letter.

Choices

- The first thing for the customer services assistant to do is to suspend emotion and to listen as calmly as possible to what he is being told. This is the only way of finding out what has occurred.

- Once the problem has been described, it is important to discover if there is a particular person or process that is to blame. For example, did someone forget to input a piece of vital information (500 items not 50 items); was the date for delivery incorrectly noted (10/01/10 instead of 01/10/10)?

- Showing sincere concern for the upset customer is helpful. The customer services assistant could saying something along the lines of 'how frustrating for you' or 'I can see how upset this mistake has made you'.

- Should it become clear that the fault lies with the person dealing with the complaint, they should have the courage to admit it, right away. Honesty is the best policy in such cases.

- Offering some sort of recompense is another option. It is necessary on the part of the customer services assistant to find out, by careful questioning, what sort of compensation would be most appropriate in the circumstances.

- If it is a serious complaint it may require handling by those superior to the customer services team. A fairly swift decision needs to be taken on this point.

Decisions

Listening helps the customer get the anger out of their system, but it requires patience and tact on the part of the customer services assistant. The customer may be so angry that it is difficult to understand what he is saying. The customer services assistant may hear a lot more than he wishes to, but it is essential for him not to get angry too. His emotions must remain in check. If he thinks he is likely to end up shouting at the customer himself, it might be sensible to ask a cool-headed colleague to assist.

Once the customer has expressed his feelings, the customer services assistant must acknowledge them and be sincerely apologetic. The customer cannot continue to be angry once he realizes that he has a sympathetic listener.

During the disclosure, it may become evident whether there is a person, or a process that is responsible for the problem. Depending on what has been discovered, if it is appropriate for the customer services assistant to accept personal responsibility for the error, this is the best course of action. Admitting blame for the problem will take the customer by surprise in most cases. It is refreshing when someone admits a fault, as so few people do.

Should the exchange have revealed that the fault lies with another member of the customer services team, passing the buck is tempting. However, it won't help the customer to hear 'I'm sorry, this has nothing to do with me, it must have been the fault of a junior colleague of mine.' Now is not the time to deal with the apportionment of blame. That issue can wait. Carrying on with sorting out the irate customer and finding a suitable solution in his best interests is what's required.

Whatever compensation is requested, the onus is on the customer services assistant to make sure it is deliverable. Over-promising and under-delivering will bring the situation back full circle if care is not taken. Check that whatever it is the customer wants (a refund, some exchange of goods, a repeat order), this can be done without further delay or cost implication to the customer.

Should the matter have turned out to be so serious, or involve such a large amount of money (a mistake costing the company thousands of pounds) it is essential to explain politely to the customer that this matter must be referred. The customer services assistant should be aware of the limits of his responsibility and not get involved in something that is way beyond his capability. The customer will be satisfied that someone in authority will be dealing with such a serious matter.

Outcomes

The emotionally intelligent customer services assistant will have shown that he is sympathetic to the aggrieved customer. His reasonable attitude and his listening skills will help dissipate the customer's anger. By being sincerely apologetic and honest about the mistake, the customer may well arrive at the point of being satisfied. Having offered a number of different suggestions for compensation or suitable remedy, the customer services assistant has done all that could be expected in the circumstances. The customer is now in the situation where he can choose what he wants to do. The customer services assistant has shown respect to the customer throughout the exchange and maintained an unemotional but professional level of commitment to finding a solution.

Conclusion

Sometimes people are advised never to admit blame when dealing with angry customers. Should the mistake involve huge amounts of value it might be sensible to take legal advice. In most cases customers will not sue if they feel they are being treated fairly. It is always better to admit mistakes and try to sort them out. In many instances a dissatisfied customer of a company, treated in an emotionally intelligent way, can turn into a satisfied one and prove an excellent referrer for future business.

A dramatic event in a company results in a PR crisis

SITUATION

The managing director of a medium-sized company learns that an accident which has seriously injured several members of his work-force could have been caused by faulty equipment. The press are hot on his heels, sniffing around the company like a pack of hyenas in for the kill. Each reporter is keen to get first bite at the story and is looking for evidence to pin the blame on him.

The press can be a blessing or a nightmare in such a situation. Handled correctly they could be brought round to take the MD's side, but the press do like someone to blame. The MD could be the scapegoat they are looking for. The MD must find ways of handling the press (and other media) so that damage limitation can be ensured.

Choices

- The MD's responsibility is to keep the press informed right from the start. What about calling a press conference? Is this something he should do or is it best to say nothing?

- When offering information to the press, how much should he give them? A full explanation, or just enough to keep them satisfied for the moment? Do they need a full account of the history of the company or just the facts?

- Is it worth being 'economical with the truth'? Does honesty pay? Is it best to say 'No comment'?

- Should he be informing his staff as well? Keeping them in the dark could encourage one or two of them to pass on information to the press that may be misleading or outdated.

- How many people should speak to the press? Should the MD be the only person or is it wise to have others interviewed who may have different viewpoints? Can outsiders influence the press?

- Is it sensible for the MD to speculate as to what happened or future events/actions? What about the financial aspects, how much is the accident likely to cost the company?

- How will the MD be judged by the public? Should he take responsibility for what has gone wrong? How should he appear at interviews – downbeat, angry or cheerful? What should he do about recompense?

Decisions

With the press conference, the MD would gain a few points by calling a conference right at the start. He could meet them outside the company gates and inform them of the up-to-date situation.

With regard to information disclosure, the fuller the explanation the MD gives, the less the press will have to dig around to get the whole story. However, he should keep the facts simple. The press will not want, or have time for, a detailed history of the company.

Also, honesty is always the best policy. Lying does nothing for the MD; history shows it is not worth the risk (eg Richard Nixon/ David Frost interviews). When a report says 'the company has declined to comment' this tends to give the impression that there must be something to hide.

In terms of keeping control, the MD may prefer to take responsibility for speaking to the press himself. If he allows other people to be interviewed there is the possibility of contradiction.

However, if the press are taking a particularly hostile stance, getting other people on your side, to speak on your behalf could be helpful. These people could be ex-employees, satisfied customers, trade association members or anyone else.

The MD would be wise to keep the whole of his workforce informed. After all, their colleagues have been injured and they will want to know how dangerous it is to keep working. If they are aware of the current situation from the MD himself they are less likely to seek to pass on erroneous information to the reporters.

It is best for the MD to stick to the facts, remain honest and open with the press, but not to indulge in speculation as to how the accident happened, or what steps he is likely to take in future. The MD must bear in mind what the public perception of the accident may be. If he says 'there's no risk to other employees' people reading the press reports may not believe him. He would be wiser to say that a full investigation is underway and all necessary precautions have been set up to protect the rest of the workforce in the meantime.

Should the MD feel the fault is his, he should do everything he can to put things right. Even in the event of the press blaming him, the right actions will go a long way to silencing critics. Announcing that he is giving the injured employees assistance with medical treatment and ensuring that their families have what help they need will show him to be a responsible and compassionate person.

Outcomes

If the MD has been fortunate enough to receive advice on handling the media, he will realize it is best not to appear too worried when giving interviews (because people will think he's in trouble), nor angry (they will take a dislike to him). If the MD strikes the right attitude, positive yet polite with the press, but sympathetic to those who have suffered injury, this will help him get a fair hearing.

He has to bear in mind that it is the press's job to deal with crises every day. His information should be jargon-free and the message clear and unambiguous. If he is confident when giving interviews, then he should be the single spokesperson. It ensures that one consistent viewpoint is put across.

Should he need it, eliciting supporting statements on behalf of the company have more credibility from outsiders than insiders. The wise MD, pressed for information he does not have, will say he doesn't know, or that there is nothing he can tell them at the moment rather than the stark 'No comment'.

Conclusion

The right way of handling the press in the face of a crisis is to stick to the priorities: first the people involved – in this case, the injured employees; secondly the safety aspects – the working environment with regard to the rest of the company personnel; thirdly any financial implications – replacing the machinery that could be at fault or closing down part of the company while investigations take place.

A team leader has problems with his team's motivation. How can he boost performance and inspire his people?

SITUATION

The team leader knows that motivation matters, yet because he is busy, he has not paid much attention to his intentions to keep his team's morale high. As a result team performance is poor and he is worried that he will be judged on their results. Every member of a team can be motivated by something. However, the team leader is mistaken if he thinks one thing will be effective across the whole team.

Choices

- A demotivated team will bring greater demands on the team leader's time. He must find time to help them otherwise this situation could get out of hand.

- He needs to take the 'motivational temperature' of the team but how often should this be done?

- He wants to take action to maintain the interest of the team members. He thinks he should be creative, but will this work?

- Evaluating what makes the team tick is important. Do they have sufficient job satisfaction and do they feel involved with the company as a whole?

- There is one problem person who does not seem to respond to the motivators that work for the rest of the team. Should this person be encouraged to stay in the team or leave it?

- The team leader knows that fun is a motivator, but how much 'fun' is it appropriate for the team to have?

Decisions

The team leader keeps the 'people' aspects firmly in mind at all times. If he is aware of his people, he will know that applying motivation 'little and often' is an effective way to maintain good performance. He is aware of all possible motivational actions – large and small – and he schedules time for 'teamwork' every week.

A 'one size fits all' policy is not the most effective. It is a big mistake to assume that everyone is motivated by the same things – for example money and status. A team leader could consider other things, such as responsibility or challenges. Motivational actions must be well judged from all the team members' perspectives.

Praise is one of the greatest motivators – whether it is said privately, publicly, in writing – it is always welcome. Recognition, appreciation and thanks when team members perform well will do wonders for morale for individuals or the team as a whole.

Job satisfaction is a key motivator. Each member of the team needs to feel they can do their part of the job well. If one or two members need training, this is the team leader's responsibility – either to train them himself or to arrange for appropriate training to be given.

Motivation will be high if each member of the team feels they are being effective.

The team should understand how their work fits into the scheme of things. Each member should be aware of why their part of the process is essential to the team as a whole, what the right actions are, and the appropriate way to carry them out. Knowing that they are an important part of the organization is desirable. The team leader should ask for their input, ideas or suggestions and *listen* to what they tell him.

The person who seems to be unmotivated despite all the team leader's efforts has a problem. So does the team leader, because this person's poor performance is affecting the rest of the team's efforts. The team leader must discover what, if anything, would make him feel more enthusiastic. If no progress is made, perhaps the team leader should suggest a move to another part of the company. There is no point in remaining part of the team if his negativity is affecting the rest of the group.

The team leader knows that devoting time to maintaining motivational levels will make the effort worthwhile. No one works well in a situation where there is 'doom and gloom'. It is always important to inject a 'fun' element into work. This could involve competitive sport, intellectual challenges, social events or a mixture.

Outcomes

The successful team leader's awareness that individually and collectively his team need to feel motivated reflects his emotional intelligence. He sees this process as continuous and cumulative. Ensuring that everyone performs well is his goal since it follows that a happy team achieves more. The team leader is also happier because he has fewer demands on his time (of a negative sort). His motivation is high because he can see the healthy attitude of his team. If everyone in the team is coping well, so will the team leader.

Conclusion

Successful team leaders are continuously motivating their team; they keep their people constantly in mind. They make motivation a habit. Their applied emotional intelligence alerts them to declining morale in others. Their awareness of the team's performance is regularly checked and they do not allow the team's motivation to decrease. Should this happen a disproportionate amount of effort would be involved to bring performance back to a satisfactory level.

A sales executive, having difficulty in reaching his targets, applies new thinking

SITUATION

Selling is not easy and at times it is difficult to reach preset targets for a variety of reasons. Once a sales executive begins to doubt his ability to close a deal, he is likely to unconsciously convey this to a prospect. A never to be repeated opportunity to achieve a sale could be lost. How can he make sure this does not happen? The sales executive who applies emotional intelligence to his selling methods will bring in better results.

Choices

- The sales executive could continue doing what he has always done. His failure to reach targets could be down to outside forces, market conditions and economic downturn.

- He could review his sales techniques to see that they are being deployed in a way that maximizes his chances of getting a positive result.

- Is he taking too long to make a sales case, does it excite the prospective purchaser or is it too introspective?

- He could look at the situation from the potential customer's point of view; what are their needs and will his product meet them?
- What about details? Too much, too little? The salesman could review the descriptions he uses: are they vague and fuzzy, or memorable, clear and match the buyer's situation?
- Does he regard selling as a one-way process, or a conversation? What merit is there in actively seeking customer involvement?

Decisions

The sales executive knows that he isn't the only person having difficulty in selling the product. He regards the way he sells as satisfactory. His product may not represent 'best value' and customers are taking longer to make decisions. He reports back to his regional manager that it is nothing to do with him.

The sales executive checks his presentation skills. He is thorough; he knows a lot about the product and wants the customer to hear all about the company, how the product evolved and what it can do. His internal viewpoint is safe ground. He knows what he knows and it creates a firm platform from which to sell.

He could focus on 'what's in it for the customer'. This could excite the prospect, who will start listening for reasons to buy. If the salesman lists the benefits to the prospect if he purchases the product – not the product's features, which are factual things – he could effect a dramatic change. Benefits include what the effect of buying from him has had on other customers (ie improves their effectiveness, reduces costs, increases productivity, strengthens their customer service).

He decides to operate from a different viewpoint. What do people want to know about what he is selling? Can they afford it and does it represent good value for money? Do they really believe what the seller is telling them? Is the product competitive (because they could be looking at several options)? He emphasizes safety and certainty as his core points.

The salesman reviews his own methods. He knows that he never buys anything unless he understands the product and the case being put for it and (most importantly) he really believes that the product will give him what he wants. He realizes that the same criteria will be used by his prospects. Successful selling is all about helping people to buy. If he can do it in a way that matches how they make decisions, and create belief as well, he will find it easier to reach his targets.

Outcomes

Adopting an 'external' sales technique rather than an 'introspective' one, the sales executive immediately differentiates himself from those who talk endlessly about themselves. The subject switches from 'him' to 'the customer'. It sparks interest early on and prompts people to adopt a positive approach to what comes next. It engages the prospect at an early stage.

Instead of saying 'so what?' when the sales executive finishes speaking, the potential customer is much more likely to become interested and begin to seek a match with their own situation as they continue to listen. They already want to know more and the salesperson can check this out as they go along: 'If that seems of interest, let me explain how it works.'

Conclusion

The sales executive who thinks through his presentation logically – based more on the way the customers buy and their thinking – is applying emotional intelligence. He does not rely on his own thoughts and convenience. The best method a sales executive can employ is to gain his prospect's attention early on and keep them interested in a constructive way. Lack of belief is probably the reason most sales meetings fail – the product looks good, but the prospect is not quite sure. Build a case by establishing a core list of benefits and what these will deliver, this approach stands the greatest chance of establishing belief.

A director has a meeting with an important client. There is a large contract to be awarded and a positive outcome is critical for his company's future prosperity. How can he control the outcome of the exchange?

SITUATION

The director is not without experience in dealing with people, but he is nervous about this meeting as a lot depends on the decision. He is a little wary of this client, who can be dominating. Because he is anxious that his company wins the deal, he wants to come across with confidence and retain control of the meeting. For the client to decide to award the contract in his favour, he must be convinced that the director is a competent person. How can the director gain an 'unfair' advantage from the start?

Choices

- The director knows he can usually handle people well. He thinks he instinctively knows how to employ his 'people skills'. He doesn't have much time to prepare for the meeting, so goes ahead without reviewing his options. He is convinced that an 'ad hoc' approach is more relaxed and shows confidence. He can go with the flow and see what happens.

- He could prepare for the meeting in advance. If preparation is the best way of controlling the outcome of a situation, how much time should be spend on it? Would a few moments thinking before starting the meeting be sufficient? Perhaps an hour or two of quiet homework would be more appropriate. He could sit down at a table with colleagues, exploring the best way forward and even rehearsing a number of possible ways things could be done.

- The director knows that impressions count. It is important how he comes across to the client. He is anxious to gain his respect and wants to appear professional and expert. He also wants to exude authority. He takes what he views as an assertive stance, to show the client that he is in control.

- The director knows that his client can be determined. Should it come to a tough decision, negotiating might gain the outcome that he desires. Negotiating skills are always useful but the director has dealt with this client before. Familiarity should make negotiation unnecessary and sometimes a willingness to negotiate can be regarded by the other party as a sign of weakness.

Decisions

The director decides to go ahead and play things by ear. At the appointed time, the client arrives in a flustered state. There is a problem at his end and he has to cut the meeting short and return to his office. The director cannot, without seeming unreasonable, insist that the meeting continues as planned. The conversation ends before it has begun. There is no opportunity to reschedule; the client says he will call to arrange another meeting.

Preparation is never a waste of time. The director spends some time thinking about the forthcoming meeting. He consults with his colleagues about the possible outcomes: they are awarded the contract; they are awarded a specific part of the contract; they are not awarded the contract at all, but perhaps they are in the frame for a different one. Could being patient pay off long-term? He has a plan of action that he can bring into play depending on the line taken by the client. He is in control because he has considered things from a 360-degree perspective.

How the client regards him is something that the director is unsure about. There is no way of finding this out; yet how he presents himself is crucial. He wants to show confidence so he spends a lot of time talking about himself, telling the client why his company should be awarded the contract. He does not allow the client much opportunity to speak and comes across as arrogant and unresponsive. This creates a one-sided effect during the meeting and conveys a negative impression. Yet the director thinks he has behaved in an impressive manner.

The director decides to put the client at ease, by behaving politely and courteously towards him. He spends time engaging the client, enquiring about the contract, what qualities the client is seeking from the company who will be awarded the contract. He asks the client to describe his 'ideal' scenario. The director employs rapport-building skills and uses mirroring techniques to emphasize a positive impression.

Negotiation is not a weak option. It requires preparation and consideration on both sides. The director knows what role he is playing and what his intention is. He also thinks about this from the client's perspective and what he may be seeking to achieve. He considers each position (subjectively and objectively). If problems arise, what objections are likely to be raised? He wants to be confident enough in his negotiating skills to ensure that things can be decided between them. This would avoid unnecessary delay such as having to consult with other parties.

Outcomes

Preparing for an important meeting has more riding on it than just one thing. The director has to identify and set specific objectives. He needs to have his priorities clearly set out and relate these to the other side's needs and objectives. He should also spend time considering his attitude to 'winning' or 'losing'. For example, does he really have to achieve everything from this one meeting? Could he employ a longer term strategy that will be of more value over a period of time? The director must be able to answer (to himself, and for his company) 'why am I doing this?' Without knowing the answer, how can he have a clear purpose? How can he control the effect on the other side and how will he recognize an ideal outcome should it be offered?

Conclusion

To be successful, the director has to use his emotional intelligence to decide his objectives. These have to be realistic, and there must be some variables. He must also have looked at the possible outcomes from the other party's viewpoint. Without putting himself in the client's shoes, he will not be able to direct the meeting confidently. Without the ability to compromise both sides will be inflexible and force a negative result, which is not the director's intention.

Delegation is the solution for the overworked accountant, but how best to achieve it?

SITUATION

An accountant has taken on a new assistant because he has so much work to do. He knows that a second person in his office should make his workload less pressured. He wants initially to delegate some routine operational tasks to her. He fears delegation could, in his profession, carry some element of risk because he will be assigning some work that is ultimately his responsibility.

The assistant is keen to take responsibility in her new job. She is anxious not to 'mess-up' otherwise she might not keep her job. Everything hinges on the accountant's ability to delegate effectively. If he succeeds, his assistant will grow in confidence, and he will be able to assign more complex tasks to her. Increasing someone's area of responsibility is an important factor in improving morale and job satisfaction. Should the accountant be emotionally aware, he will be able to develop the skills to become a good delegator.

Choices

- The accountant knows he is really overwhelmed with work so he employs a new assistant. However, the accountant feels that nobody can actually do any of the work but him so continues to do everything himself.

- He realizes he has to save time. But does he have time to delegate? The accountant tells his assistant what he wants her to do. He chooses a routine task, which is boring and tedious, puts some papers on her desk and leaves her to it.

- His new assistant is keen and capable. He could delegate some work to her that involves decision-making skills. If she is successful, this could make him feel insecure.

- There are certain tasks that the accountant enjoys doing. He knows it is something that could easily be delegated to his assistant, but he carries on doing it himself.

- Planning to delegate a complex task to his assistant, the accountant thinks about what he wants done, and how best his assistant could carry it out. He briefs his assistant, sets a review date and checks that she has understood what he has said.

- The accountant is so pleased with his new assistant he decides to give her more work involving strategy and business planning.

Decisions

Working with the new assistant is something the accountant is unfamiliar with. The accountant is too busy working to give her anything to do. She sits around and wonders why she is there at all. The fear of delegating is too great for the accountant; he feels this will reduce his control and place reliance on his assistant who may prove inadequate.

The accountant starts by delegating a routine task to his new assistant. He doesn't have much time, and delegates the work badly.

The new assistant is nervous, confused and doesn't understand exactly what her boss is saying. Things quickly go wrong. The accountant gets cross, removes the job from her and grumbles that 'it's easier to do it myself'. He fails to understand that delegation requires clear and unambiguous instructions.

The assistant is given a task that involves a degree of responsibility. It requires her to make some decisions that she is well qualified and has the skills to do. She makes good progress but her boss does not praise or thank her. Despite the fact that he wants her to take increased responsibility, he refuses to pass similar work to her as he begins to feel threatened by her competence.

The accountant is doing something that his assistant is capable of handling. Unfortunately, the accountant enjoys this particular task and is unwilling to hand it over to her. His reluctance to delegate is blocking the assistant's progress; tasks that are unpleasant to the delegator are not the only ones that should be delegated.

Having taken time to plan the job he is delegating, the accountant feels in control of the situation. He shows confidence in his assistant and she responds positively. The briefing goes smoothly and the assistant checks that she has understood his instructions and the date by which the work is to be completed. She takes responsibility for the whole job and does not let him down.

There are some tasks that should not be delegated. The accountant should retain all jobs involving strategy and planning, as he is the person to set these aims and objectives. He wants to grow the practice and take on more staff in future but these decisions should be his alone.

Outcomes

The accountant must learn to delegate effectively: while he believes the risks of delegation outweigh the potential rewards he will not make progress.

Effective delegation develops the assistant's skills, which helps the accountant to get more done. The bonus for the delegate is that it is fast-tracking her towards a higher level of responsibility. The accountant and the assistant both have a responsibility to ensure that the delegated task is done well.

The accountant sees the potential shown by his assistant, but he risks losing control by delegating tasks above and beyond her capabilities. Strategic decision-making tasks are not among the jobs that should be delegated.

Conclusion

Of course delegating is risky, and a task may not be done well to begin with. But that is no reason to refuse to delegate. The job should be done properly, but an effective delegator allows staff to perform tasks in a way that suits their personality and way of working.

There are certain tasks that should be delegated and there are some that should not. The delegator should be able to distinguish between them.

Effective delegating is not only a time saver (in the long run) but it also an excellent way of coaching or training the delegate. Allow the delegate the freedom to interpret the manner of carrying out the work. Emotional intelligence helps the delegator decide which tasks are appropriate for delegation and the best way of encouraging the delegate to accept responsibility for them. He must think beyond his own needs to those of the delegate and ensure that as many of them as possible are met through effective delegation.

Overcoming office politics with emotional intelligence

SITUATION

The facilities manager in a company holds a responsible position. He manages some large premises, and is accountable for security and services. Yet because his character is not loud or bombastic some of his colleagues regarded him as little more than the guy in charge of the stationery cupboard. He is not much good at office politics and doesn't act assertively as a matter of course. Some survival strategies would assist him. In a political environment such as the workplace, power, authority and control are things everyone craves. The facilities manager has more authority than he realizes and is being too modest. How can he use his skills to advantage if he doesn't realize his strengths?

Choices

- The facilities manager thinks he can't play office politics. He wants to be more assertive with some of his disparaging colleagues. Because he doesn't know how to do this, he finds it easier to accept what they say and put up with it.

- When he considers it, the facilities manager knows he has many good qualities, strengths and skills. He would not hold the job he does if he was ineffective. How can he motivate himself to boost his self-image?

- Attitude matters and the facilities manager seeks to influence his critics positively towards him. When an IT crisis occurs in the office panic ensues. The colleagues search for someone to help who has the necessary skills and information. One of the facilities manager's responsibilities is operating the various computer back-up systems that the company uses. Unfortunately his co-workers don't rate him highly enough to ask if he can help.

Decisions

The facilities manager doesn't possess a self-awareness checklist. He isn't strong on self-analysis or sure of his strengths and weaknesses. His lack of action keeps him in a passive/negative frame of mind and the colleagues continue to taunt him. The problem in doing nothing to redress a situation is that it encourages the co-workers to think they are right in their opinion.

The HR department carry out appraisals annually on every member of staff. The facilities manager decides to review his last appraisal, which shows his particular skills, his personality factors and his knowledge of his job, responsibilities and the organization. The facilities manager builds up a checklist of his attributes: his past experience (previous jobs and positions he held); his skills (with figures, people and project management); his expertise (ability to make sound decisions). He feels better about himself, which gives him greater self-confidence.

As a solution provider for various aspects of the company, the facilities manager has the necessary information, knows how to implement a plan of action and can put it into operation right away. He decides to go over the heads of the unreasonable colleagues and approach one of the directors to advise him that he can solve the IT issue if he is given permission. The facilities manager is given the go ahead to proceed by the director. The crisis is solved without further delay or loss of time and money. The director advises the other staff that the matter has been dealt with effectively by the facilities manager and asks them why they hadn't sought his advice in the first place.

Outcomes

Because the facilities manager was aware that he had the power to solve the crisis, he did not hesitate to approach the director. He had a plan of action at the ready and the self-confidence to implement it when given the authority to do so. As a result the director was able to influence the co-workers that in future the facilities manager is someone worth approaching on matters about which they have less experience.

Conclusion

Once the facilities manager had worked out his personal strengths, he was in a more confident frame of mind. When faced with an opportunity, he was able to make an assertive decision that had a beneficial outcome for himself, his colleagues and his company. It is emotionally intelligent for the facilities manager to take control of a situation if he is equipped to do so, rather than leave things to get worse.

Staff appraisal interviews can be fraught with difficulty

SITUATION

Managers approach appraising their staff with anxiety. It is a serious issue and an important opportunity to ensure good performance in the coming year. Appraisals are designed to pinpoint the current level of employee competence and highlight any areas that need attention, such as training and mentoring. The process can be an awkward one if the manager is not confident about his abilities to conduct appraisals. It is a source of stress to the member of staff if the appraisal offers no practical benefit or satisfaction. Good appraisals do not just happen.

Choices

- Staff appraisals are a three-stage process: before the interview, during the interview, and the follow-up period. It is important that these stages are all conducted properly, bearing in mind that it is a two-way process.

- The manager is responsible for preparing for the meeting, setting the agenda and checking the documentation.

- During the interview there are a number of sensitive issues that need to be discussed. Should these be dealt with or should they be shelved to avoid peer embarrassment?

- In his anxiety and nervousness about the appraisal process, the manager spends a lot of the meeting talking to the staff member about his past performance. The manager can set targets and other objectives to the relevant period under review and he can also set out the processes to be followed during the ensuing months.

Decisions

It is essential not only for the manager but also the employee to understand how the appraisal system works in their organization. Once the meeting has started it is too late to find this out so self-preparation is important. One way to find out is to ask colleagues and peers how they felt their appraisals were conducted.

Before the appraisal meeting can take place the manager must set an agenda, arrange for the appropriate documentation to be available (and read) by both parties and have a clear estimate of the time it should take. If he does not ensure that any of the above is dealt with, the meeting could be less than effective on both sides.

Unless both parties are resolved to deal with whatever issues are necessary, openly and honestly, the appraisal interview will be invalid. Criticism is part of an appraisal process but should be given constructively. The purpose of this is that if it is accepted in the right way, it should be directly linked to development and training, which should lead to enhanced employee performance.

The process of appraisal should allow a member of staff to feel able to talk freely. The appraiser may need to steer the direction of the discussion but he should not dominate the meeting. The member of staff should focus on his future, not on the past experience of the recent months; the manager should do the same. It should be a positive opportunity for the employee to present his competencies so that they are recorded.

During the meeting, the manager may choose to ignore the facts. He may not focus on the targets and objectives set during the period under review. He makes judgements that are unsupported by documentation, based on hearsay or uncertain memory. He sets the scene for an uncomfortable exchange and a less than productive encounter next time.

Outcomes

The appraisal conducted from the manager's limited range of experience is valueless. It does not offer the member of staff much opportunity for constructive reflection and growth. The manager has not realized that listening is more important than talking. He has failed to view the process as two-way and has not put himself into the mindset of the member of staff.

The process is as unhelpful to him as it is to the employee; and the company as well. Approached in the right way, this is one of the manager's greatest opportunities to create good future performance. Due to his lack of emotional intelligence he may well waste it. Adequate training should be given to managers who are expected to conduct staff appraisals to ensure that they are capable of making the most of an extremely important process which impacts in a number of ways across the company.

Conclusion

The manager in his dislike of conducting staff appraisals has never grasped the fundamental point of the process. It is a two-way operation. It should be conducted with emphasis on the positive not the negative aspects of the staff member's abilities, and focus on the future not past actions that have taken place. It should be a satisfying experience for the manager and the employee – not an ordeal.

Chapter 10
Emotional intelligence and the personal situations you face

This section is about people who, for one reason or another, may be awkward, unreasonable or in some other way, not quite so easy to deal with. It explores what you might be able to do with them or about them.

Dealing with bullies: the marketing manager of a company is presenting his strategy for business development to the board of directors

SITUATION

His managing director asks to see the strategy before the meeting. The MD looks through the document and shakes his head. 'The Board will never approve this. It's rubbish.' The marketing manager is completely taken aback. He politely rejects the MD's criticism by explaining that the document has been checked by the finance, sales and other relevant departments. The MD explodes with anger, tells the marketing manager to get out and says that it's of no interest who has approved the strategy. He doesn't agree with it so it's got to be redone. His final remark to the marketing manager is that he must come up with something better quickly or he'll be out of a job.

Destructive, hostile, aggressive people live to dominate, insult and wound others. People like this often take issue not only with someone's work, but also someone's behaviour and reactions. When set in motion, they can be like steamrollers and carry on crushing anything that comes into their path. Once destructive people realize how much they can terrorize those who work with them, they get worse. They are impossible to deal with, and are usually angry. The only way they feel they can get something from another person is through threats and criticism and they behave like this throughout an entire organization. It seems that the only way they can feel 'big' is by making others feel 'small'. This can be the result of them having been bullied at some time themselves; bullies often have low self-esteem.

Choices

- In the mind of the marketing manager are several different courses of action.

- He can do exactly what he's been asked to do by the unreasonable MD. Redo the work and hope his amended strategy is more acceptable.

- He could do absolutely nothing. The no-response reaction is likely to take the MD by surprise. Holding a no-response position gives nothing away.

- He could stand his ground and refuse to accept what the MD has said. This could throw the MD off track because he is used to intimidating people to get what he wants. The marketing manager might lose his temper with the MD.

- The marketing manager could attempt to take control of the situation by means of assertive behaviour.

Decisions

The marketing manager has a choice of four possible options.

If he accepts that the MD is right, and his presentation is worthless, he is capitulating to a bully. He will become stressed, work late each evening and over the weekend to produce a new document in time for the MD to see it before the board meeting. He has no idea whether this piece of new work will be any more acceptable to the unreasonable MD than the previous strategy document.

The marketing manager could do absolutely nothing. He would need to disengage his emotions and behave in an uncharacteristic way. (Most bullies expect to get a reaction – usually one of craven obedience.) The no-response reaction is not what they expect and can deter them. The marketing manager stands up straight, remains in the MD's office, takes a deep breath and does nothing. The cooler and more unaffected he appears, the greater this will upset the unreasonable MD. Holding his position of no action buys him some time. The MD, seeing he is deprived of his usual satisfaction (watching people creep away utterly humiliated) finds this situation worrying. The marketing manager, by showing no signs of being wounded, has confused the MD who doesn't know what to do next.

The marketing manager could use guerrilla tactics and fight back. After all, he hasn't been dealt with in a civilized manner so he could retaliate by attacking the MD and telling him exactly what he thinks of him. This course of action could escalate to the point where they have a shouting match. Nothing is resolved satisfactorily and the marketing manager has fallen into a trap set by the bullying MD, which he may later regret.

The option of making a case for himself is another possibility. The marketing manager behaves in an assertive way and points out, politely, to the MD that he clearly has looked through the document in great haste, perhaps he hasn't understood it fully. He could offer to go through the document with him in detail. Should anything stand out that doesn't seem clear, he could then explain the section to the MD. The marketing manager by asserting himself is taking the best course of action for him, given the lack of time available before the board meeting. He could point out, assertively, that in practical terms the document cannot be 'reworked' before the meeting, but if needed some minor amendments could be made that might be more in line with the MD's thinking.

Outcomes

The emotionally intelligent response to bullies depends on the circumstances of the encounter. In this instance the marketing manager wants to arrive at a situation where he can be seen to be responsive to the MD's demands despite their unreasonable nature. Being passive and agreeing that the work is useless and should be redone doesn't work. The no-action reaction could work but the outcome cannot be guaranteed. It is sometimes worth playing the non-aggressive stand just to call a bully's bluff. The fighting-back reaction is probably the most natural but perhaps not the wisest course of action. Situations where tempers are raised can get out of hand. The marketing manager is well advised to attempt to regain control of a situation that has turned into a nightmare scenario. If he can persuade the MD to review the document and to point out the areas he doesn't accept, the marketing manager has the greatest chance of pushing through the strategy without further work or, perhaps, with only minor alterations.

Dealing with bullies of whatever sort requires strong nerves and a sense of purpose. If they are allowed to behave unchecked, they get worse. Once a person has made a stand against them, they often bluster and go away. It is important to be sure of your own ground before taking on a bully, but it is worth the attempt. The person with good self-esteem and the ability to assert themselves will be able to turn the tables on a destructive, aggressive person.

Conclusion

The emotionally intelligent marketing manager has to think quickly and decisively about what will be the best win–win situation. He doesn't agree that his strategy document is worthless, but he does want to retain his job. The MD is clearly being unreasonable so how can the marketing manager get him to see sense without making him lose face? The assertive, positive approach is helpful to the MD; not disrespectful, but firm. This should give the best outcome.

Blamers, complainers and irresponsible people. The most recent member of staff to join the department has poor timekeeping skills

SITUATION

The team leader quite reasonably asks the new member of staff if she would make more effort to be punctual. He points out that it is quite noticeable and it is important that everyone gets to the office on time. She at once explains that it's not her fault. The bus is often held up in traffic. She sometimes gets delayed leaving the house. And anyway her timekeeping has never been criticized before in previous jobs. The team leader politely asks her to make sure she arrives on time in future.

People who are irresponsible and who blame others for things that happen are difficult to deal with. Their behaviour is unacceptable because they do not accept responsibility. They are fully paid up members of the 'half-empty glass club'. Their usual reaction to any criticism is 'it wasn't my fault'. If a piece of equipment breaks while they are using it, it was nothing to do with them. They are full of blame, accusations, protestations of innocence, suggestions of injustice and pessimism. While they may not openly antagonize colleagues, they can drive co-workers to distraction by their response to remarks, situations and requests for action. People who are complainers or blamers find it hard to accept responsibility for what they've done. They seldom apologize and the net result is a dissipation of positive energies across the workplace even from upbeat and reasonable colleagues.

Choices

- The team leader has a number of possible actions.

- He can insist that the staff member arrives on time every morning, otherwise he will be forced to take disciplinary action against her.

- He can instigate a new office procedure that may make a difference to her behaviour.

- He can listen to her grievances and try to understand the reasons why she is always late for work and offer possible solutions.

- He can suggest she assumes responsibility for her actions so that she can effect a change in her behaviour. In effect, he lays down a challenge.

Decisions

The team leader must do something otherwise the situation will not get better and the other members of staff will become more resentful of the new person's behaviour.

He asks the new member of staff to make sure she is on time every day. He allows her no options. If her timekeeping doesn't improve, he will discipline her. If she makes no effort, she will eventually lose her position because of her inability to adhere to one of the terms of her conditions of employment. This will be entirely the employee's fault, not the firm attitude taken by the team leader.

He introduces an attendance register, which every member of staff in his department has to fill in on arrival and on departure with the date and the time. This demonstrates to the poor-timekeeper that the team leader means business. It also shows that he is being fair to the rest of his staff. If they are capable of getting to work on time, why shouldn't it be recorded? It will be in black and white every morning and he can check the facts without having to rely on the word of anyone else. This might shame her into getting to work on time.

He decides to listen, with patience, to the excuses the new member of staff gives for her poor timekeeping. He empathizes and shows he understands her situation. He offers two or three sensible solutions (she catches an earlier bus, she drives to work, she leaves the house in good time by getting up earlier). He is trying to establish whether the poor-timekeeper actually does want to change things. If her response to all suggestions is that she couldn't possibly do any of them, none of this is her fault and the team leader clearly doesn't understand her problems, it will be difficult to move forward. If he persists, he may get the employee to accept the situation she is in. If she admits it, then he must make it clear that she has the ability to change and take control of her actions. No one can be both in control and a victim. Once the team leader can get that message through to her, he may have achieved success with this employee.

The team leader offers the member of staff a challenge. He tries to provoke her into action so that her viewpoint is changed. He interrupts her forcibly when she begins to recite the reasons why it is not her fault that she cannot get to work on time. He could raise his voice or use gestures to stop her talking. He points out to her that when she is at work she is excellent at her job and could be in line for a transfer/promotion in future. However, nothing like that will be possible unless she can prove to him that she is able to take responsibility. The way to start is for her to accept responsibility for her weak timekeeping and get to the office punctually along with her colleagues.

Dealing with people who are irresponsible, blamers or complainers requires firm handling. No one should be allowed to get away with substandard behaviour at work as it is not fulfilling the terms and conditions of the contract. Also it is the quickest way of spreading negativity across any department.

Outcomes

Complainers are forever victims. Irresponsible people are extremely annoying. If the team leader suggests that something they have done needs improving, they switch to martyr mode instantly. Standing firm could provoke a range of reactions, tears, sighs and sulks, which if left unchecked will have repercussions around the entire department. The team leader must maintain good morale through-out his department. He cannot allow the behaviour of one member of staff to change the departmental atmosphere.

Conclusion

Dealing with complainers and other negative types requires patience. Listening to them and helping them to take a positive and responsible attitude for their action assumes that the team leader is able to take a neutral and objective viewpoint. That may not work and he may have to offer the staff member a 'take it or leave it' solution. Whatever he chooses to do, his overall goal is to have a happy and united department.

People who are uncommunicative, unresponsive and silent. A website designer comes up with a concept for a new client's site and seeks approval from his account manager

SITUATION

After running through the proposition, he waits for his comment. And waits, and waits. In exasperation he asks, 'Will you please tell me what you think?' An unreceptive boss is exasperating. He should be giving a clear answer, or at least an explanation of what he's thinking. A mumbled 'Well, er, um... ' is less than helpful. A lack of information under these circumstances can be so frustrating. The boss may have retreated behind a wall of silence in order to express disappointment or some other negative emotion. A boss or colleague who remains stubbornly unresponsive can be hard to deal with. The reasons why someone is unable to respond when required are varied. How does the website designer get the account manager to open up?

Choices

- The website designer can do any of the following.
- He can take the view that the account manager is hiding something from him and he needs to find out what is wrong.
- He can assume that he is the victim of resentment, that the account manager doesn't 'do' praise; certainly not with subordinates.
- The designer is an enthusiastic proactive person. The account manager doesn't register any emotion so the designer takes the view that the man is boring or bored.

Decisions

The designer could be right in applying any of the following lines of thought.

Because the account manager clammed up to avoid conversation, it is easy for the designer to assume there is something to hide. Perhaps he has 'messed up' and the account manager wishes at all costs to avoid a painful confrontation. Refusal to answer a question or giving a monosyllabic reply allows the account manager to avoid telling the truth. The website designer may be dealing with someone who can't tell a lie. The designer will have no idea what a conflict this is causing for the account manager. But even silence conveys a message. The designer assumes something is seriously wrong. He should show that he is patient, and wait. Eventually the account manager will say something.

The designer should stay calm, when faced with a non-response from his account manager. The boss could be stubbornly silent because he is reluctant to heap praise on the designer, whose job he feels it is to produce brilliant results every time. The designer may take the view: 'Why am I being treated like this, what have I done?' The unresponsive boss is not going to explain his motives and feelings towards the designer. He may be someone who is reluctant to treat others with respect. Should he get to know the designer better over time and appreciate his qualities, this could result in the account manager behaving more openly towards him. For the moment, the designer should not be embarrassed by the silence. He should remain sincerely inquisitive but polite, and maintain this approach whenever dealing with this person.

The designer doesn't know the account manager well but he has had positive reactions from his colleagues to his design concept. He is disappointed that the account manager won't respond but assumes the man is either incapable of communicating or just isn't into creativity. The problem could lie in the designer being a 'visual' communicator and the account manager preferring a more auditory style of communication. They use different senses to communicate. The account manager finds it very difficult to be responsive to something that is purely visual and the designer has not given any commentary or explanation as he showed the project design.

Outcomes

The designer is faced with the unenviable task of dealing with an uncommunicative boss. He may from the silent treatment be justified in thinking that something is wrong with his design. He assumes the account manager is so upset that he doesn't want to say anything. The designer must try to encourage his boss to speak, by assuring him that his opinion is essential, and that he can handle criticism. The designer could seek help from his colleagues. If they say that the account manager is always like this, the designer may feel it is less 'his fault' and that the reserved behaviour is normal from him. He should continue trying to obtain responses from his account manager but he may have to exert extreme patience in the process.

Uncommunicative people could be reluctant to speak for various reasons. Most workplaces have their silent types. Some people don't speak unless they feel they have something to say. They don't regard remaining silent as being unhelpful. They will speak if they wish to. Other people who don't respond readily could be reticent and shy or bored. They will require a lot of encouragement to enter into conversations. Whatever the cause of their lack of response, it requires a lot of patience and commitment from colleagues to open up communication channels. The alternative is to leave them alone and they will find themselves excluded.

Conclusion

If the designer has tried all manner of techniques for eliciting information from his account manager but failed, the best way forward is to show him that he has a real interest in his opinion. The unresponsive boss may be sensitive and prefer to protect himself behind a wall of silence. He will be highly attuned to any form of insincerity, so whatever technique the designer employs to get some dialogue going, it must be genuine.

Competitive people. A manager has to cope with a challenging member of staff

SITUATION

The manager has a good group of staff apart from one, who turns every workplace situation into a competition that he has to win. The competitive person likes to be centre stage, have the last word on things, produce the best results and be involved in every decision. It is exhausting for his colleagues because they don't feel the need to compete. It is tiring for the manager who has to keep intervening to keep this overactive manipulator in check.

Choices

- The manager wants his department to run smoothly. It is essential for him to deal effectively with this competitive employee.

- The competitive staff member presents a challenge to the manager. The manager could, if he chooses, turn the tables and give him a challenge on every available occasion.

- He could offer regular office challenges and ensure that the competitive member of staff doesn't take all the prizes.

- He could motivate his staff in different ways to suit the individuals. The competitive staff member would receive his motivation in the form of contests while the others would be encouraged in other ways.

Decisions

The manager decides to take on the competitor at his own game. To keep him tested he sets a series of tasks for him and offers them as challenges. The manager delegates the first task to the competitive employee with the suggestion that it might perhaps be a difficult one to solve; the next task he describes as not knowing even if it is possible; a third task he presents to him because there's nobody else he can think of who could tackle it. The competitive employee grabs the chance to show his manager how capable he is.

The manager devises a series of competitions so that all members of staff feel involved. The results could be measured in different ways, to ensure that a broad range of winners is chosen. The manager could then publicly praise everyone who has obtained a prize, but explain the different criteria. For example, these could include: the most innovative solution; the best attitude to problem solving; the most effective way of working; the most helpful person in the group; the most financially viable solution.

The manager spends some time working on a variety of motivational issues for the whole department. He interviews each member of staff to ascertain which way they prefer to be motivated. He makes sure that the competitive member of staff is effectively challenged as well.

Outcomes

The competitive employee accepts every challenge thrown at him by his manager. He thinks that by taking these jobs on, he is the winner. The manager can praise him publicly or privately, but the employee is most likely to enjoy having praise heaped on him in front of his colleagues. In the mixed office challenge, the competitive employee ploughs ahead hoping to scoop the pool of prizes.

The emotionally intelligent manager has worked out a number of criteria for 'winning' that play to the strengths of other staff in the department. He praises them all publicly. For the general good health of the department the manager organizes a motivational mix to inspire all his staff.

The manager knows that there are some people who not only crave attention, they also love to have challenges and contests, so that they can win. This staff member thrives on winning even though none of his colleagues are bothered about keeping up with him.

Conclusion

Competitive staff can be exhausting. They are always out to prove something: what skills they have; their knowledge of the job; their connections and contacts. They can be described by colleagues as 'difficult' to work with. Every employee has strengths: their experience (previous jobs and positions they've held); their skill (with figures, people or projects); their expertise (ability to make good decisions, solve problems, know which products to promote). But not everyone wants to be 'first'. Employees who are confident about themselves and what they are doing don't feel the need to compete. The competitive person has deep insecurities, and doesn't feel satisfied unless he has beaten someone into second place – even when there isn't a race taking place.

Disruptive people. Personality clashes within a team

SITUATION

A department has a reputation for putting together effective teams. The latest group chosen to work on a project includes some strong personalities. Their behaviour is threatening to disrupt the rest of the group. Two individuals have personality clashes and each is attempting to pull the team in a different direction. If allowed to continue unchecked, it will destabilize the entire team and affect the running of the project.

Choices

- The team leader could call the whole team together to re-establish the focus of the project, its needs and objectives.

- He could invite the two team members together to a meeting and mediate while they discuss their disagreements.

- In talking through their differences, the team leader emphasizes that the focus is on the issues, not the personalities involved.

- The team leader states that the meeting cannot finish without an agreement about their future behaviour.

- He could arrange a review date to see how things progress and thank them for co-operating in trying to resolve the problem.

Decisions

Accepting that these two strong personalities have conflicting ideas and are likely to damage the team's effectiveness, the team leader should initially gather the whole team together to refocus them on their objectives. He could explain how different aims, styles of working and ambitions will prevent the team from progressing as it should.

He should call a meeting with the two people. If he talks to them individually, each will wonder what was said to the other. They could even misrepresent the team leader to each other, which could cause a three-way conflict. The purpose of meeting them together is to get them to sort out their issues, not to allocate blame.

The team leader makes it clear that if any points cannot be resolved between them they must accept his decision on them. These decisions can always be reviewed later if difficulties persist.

The team leader should set out rules, such as to allow each member to finish what they are saying without interruption. The focus should be firmly on the problem, not their personalities. They should be encouraged to talk about their own feelings and reactions rather than focusing on the other person's actions.

Outcomes

The team leader should have a flexible approach and be a helpful and supportive member of the group. A committed team understands the importance of the project. Success depends on understanding the objective and making sure that the team operates as a united front.

The successful team leader is capable of establishing productive working relationships and dealing with conflict. Being part of a team requires every member to take responsibility to work harmoniously with the rest of the group. Where there is no trust among team members, or where conflicts arise because of forceful personalities, the team will not function well. Unless steps are taken to resolve disputes, huge amounts of energy will be used in solving conflicts, resulting in loss of time and creativity.

Conclusion

Creating a productive team is an essential skill; effective teams produce far more than people working individually. Good teamwork demands emotional intelligence to help create group motivation. A team cannot function well while coping with the activities of disruptive members. Teams require support, from each other as well as from the leader. Any team action requires evaluation, so a review plan should be established. A team leader should be unstinting in giving praise. Should failures occur, he should make sure the lessons learned are positive and constructive. Finally team members should be given the opportunity of appraisal of their performance. Guidance and training should be offered if team members wish it.

Angry, hostile, unreasonable people. A manager finds his staff are rebellious and unsupportive

SITUATION

Colleagues who are angry and hostile can come across in different ways. Anger can be direct as a result of something said or done; or it can be cold, plotted over a longer period of time. In a department the conduct of others corrodes the atmosphere quickly. A manager must discover why his staff are unsupportive of him and address the problem.

Choices

- The manager could look to his management style.
- He could check whether he is unpopular for reasons outside of his control.
- He could try winning the support of each individual member of the department by getting to know his staff, and become more than 'the manager'.

Decisions

Management styles differ widely. This manager may be guilty of poor management style. He should check that he is fair, trustworthy, positive, able to communicate, supportive and organized. He could go one step further and let his staff know that he would appreciate constructive comment. After all, his staff may need to tell him how he can get the best performance from them.

The manager may be unpopular for reasons he knows nothing about. It is possible that the staff wanted someone else for the job; or he was promoted from a part of the organization they are particularly hostile to. He could talk to them all explaining the reasons he has been given for his appointment and ask for their support.

The manager could work on each individual member of staff. If he manages to win the trust of one or two of his staff, the rest may follow suit. This is not to say he should bribe his way into his staff's affection by giving them 'perks', but get to know them as people. This should dispel any anger or hostility directed towards him.

If some members of staff are particularly angry they could be talked to individually to ascertain the reasons. The manager should acknowledge their feelings while explaining his own position. He should make it clear that he wants to put things right by listening to them. But the important thing is to move things forward by putting the angry or hostile attitude in the past.

Outcomes

When people show anger or hostility towards others there is usually a reason. It requires patience and tact to discover what is behind staff behaving in such a way. Although it is easy to take it personally, it is not always the fault of the individual. However, management style should be taken into consideration in case it is a contributory factor. The reason could be that the staff were hoping for someone else to be given the job, or that they don't like the department the manager came from. In this case the staff need reassurance, both in a group and individually, that if they wish to come to him with constructive comments, he is happy to hear them. It could be a matter of talking to individual members of staff because they are showing open hostility or anger towards him. In this case he must respect their feelings but make it clear that their attitude is upsetting the other members of staff and things have to change.

Conclusion

If one person in a department is angry about something, but the rest are calm, it isn't a great cause for concern. But should a significant proportion of staff be hostile to a manager or to each other, the situation needs sorting out, quickly. The best way of discovering the cause is to show that the angry person's feelings are acknowledged and listen to the reasons they give for their behaviour.

Moody, temperamental, jealous people. Colleagues should be able to get along together. Sometimes there are bound to be upsets, but someone who has changeable moods is difficult to build rapport with

SITUATION

Moody people are temperamental, unpredictable and unreliable. They are hard work when they are among colleagues. They are unsettling to be around, particularly in the workplace, because it is difficult to predict how they are going to react. They may be happy today and miserable tomorrow. Their mood swings may be due to being under pressure.

Choices

- Co-workers could show sympathy towards their temperamental colleagues.

- They could try engaging them in conversation in an attempt to get them to explain what is causing their stress.

- If a colleague is particularly unreasonable, it is worth asking if it is something that has happened as a result of someone else's actions. Is it a case of professional jealousy?

Decisions

A friendly gesture from another colleague to someone who is moody or unpredictable can speak volumes. It pays to be sensitive as they may be having difficulty keeping control of their emotions.

The offer to have a chat with a colleague who is under stress may be helpful. If someone says 'Has this anything to do with me? Was it something I did or said?' it opens the way for explanation. Should it turn out that it was nothing to do with another person in the office, this removes the responsibility from co-workers. The temperamental colleague should be able to explain his problems and get things out into the open.

One reason for temperamental behaviour is professional jealousy. A colleague could feel that others are doing really well at work and he is not. Job jealousy is not unusual and many people suffer from it when they think their co-workers are undermining their success or progress. One way of tackling it is to talk to the person explaining that there is a lot of tension about and ask if everything is ok. They may reply along the lines of 'I don't know what you're talking about'.

If the situation persists, a further, more assertive exchange will have to take place. The manager may need to be called in to explain the difficulties under which colleagues are placed when trying to work with the particular individual.

Outcomes

When sympathetic gestures are extended to a moody or unpredictable colleague they may not be accepted. It is important to hesitate before rushing ahead asking for explanations as to their behaviour. Colleagues are not necessarily willing to confide in others unless they trust them. Should conversation be possible, co-workers could help their troubled colleague by checking that the behaviour is not triggered by something that has happened in the office. If it is as a result of another colleague's actions, this should be dealt with as swiftly and tactfully as possible. If their difficult behaviour is due to stress from another source it may be possible to get the colleague to unburden themselves, in which case progress can be made.

If a colleague is exhibiting signs of professional jealousy, it requires a considered approach. There may be justification for their behaviour or it may be irrational. Depending on how their jealousy is shown (the odd forgotten message, or mislaid written instruction, to outright obstruction or rudeness) it is important for colleagues to focus on what is important and ignore what is trivial. Confrontation is essential. If no progress is made, colleagues have no choice but to make a complaint along formal lines. Disciplinary action may follow but since there is little chance of establishing trust and rapport with such a work colleague, there is scarcely any choice.

Conclusion

It is usually best to put on kid gloves when dealing with unpredictable colleagues. It may not work but it is sensible to start softly. Being sympathetic and encouraging them to talk can alleviate departmental tantrums. Quite often a problem shared is a problem halved. However, there are times when being nice just won't work. If it is a situation where professional jealousy is at the root of the behaviour, this will have to be tackled. The rest of the staff cannot be subjected to someone's difficult behaviour as it will have a detrimental effect on their motivation and effectiveness. However bad the situation is, colleagues should remain professional and work through the difficulty without causing further disruption to the department.

Late taskers, last-minuters. When staff work well together things tend to go smoothly. But someone who cannot work to a deadline can cause problems throughout the workplace

SITUATION

This colleague is no trouble until there's a deadline. Then he hits the panic button and there is chaos all over the department. He knows he should have started his work earlier but he didn't. In the ensuing rush he pleads with everyone to pitch in and help him finish the presentation that should have been completed days ago. In the interests of the company and because of loyalty to colleagues people rally round to dig the late tasker out of the hole he's got himself into. They insist it should be a one-off gesture, which he promises them it will be, until the next time...

Choices

- His co-workers don't want the late tasker's failure to produce work to reflect badly on them. They agree to help him out – just this once.
- Colleagues know this guy is going to ignore any deadline he is given. It comes as no surprise when he cries for help. They decide to say no to his pleas.
- They refer the problem to their manager who talks to the late tasker.

Decisions

The late tasker has appealed for help from his colleagues. They feel it is more important to the overall success of the team that they pitch in to help him complete his assignment. One or two colleagues abandon their own work, stay late and work with the late tasker to finish the job. The others take over their colleagues' work as well as their own, so that the project doesn't fall behind. This loyalty is admirable, but it does not give the late tasker any incentive to mend his ways. The team unanimously decide that this is the last time they will help him out.

The team know that one member cannot keep to deadlines. They have been caught out before. They decide when he sounds the alarm once more, as they know he will, to ignore his pleas and get on with their own work. The late tasker weeps, wails and cajoles to no effect. He has to scramble as best he can to get his work done on time. It is obvious when the work is presented to the client that it is not up to standard and lets the whole of the project down.

The team have had enough and go to their manager. He calls the late tasker in to see him. He sets out the situation clearly: that his behaviour cannot continue as it is unfair to his colleagues. In future he will be given a series of 'false' deadlines. At each stage the late tasker must show the manager the progress of his assignment. This removes the 'surprise' element that the late tasker can present to his colleagues at the last possible moment.

Outcomes

Late taskers boast that they work best when under pressure. There's nothing wrong with someone giving themselves the maximum thinking time to complete an assignment, as long as they allow sufficient time to produce the goods by the deadline. They must be sure of completing the task unaided. But frequently their claims are unrealistic and they cannot finish the job. Then late taskers rely on other people to help out when they are about to fail. This is extremely stressful if everyone else in a team has prepared well ahead of time and their own work is on schedule.

Conclusion

Late taskers need to be given the relevant facts. They should be given secondary deadlines – say a 'rehearsal' in front of the whole team two days before the work is to be presented. They need a combination of verbal and written communication as prompts to keep them clearly focused and on schedule. Sometimes it is the fear of a job being so large that prevents people beginning it in sufficient time. They may have difficulty in breaking a task into separate stages and allocating the appropriate amount of time required for each stage. It can be that some people prefer to feel increasing energy and excitement as they work closer to a deadline. Whatever the cause, the late tasker would benefit from some help with his time management.

Unrealistic, impractical people who over-promise and under-deliver

SITUATION

How can a client best deal with a supplier who is so anxious to please, or clinch an order, that he makes claims that are impossible to deliver? When a supplier over-promises, or makes claims that sound too good to be true, it is easy to accept what he says. He could be someone who just wants to be helpful. But it is anything but helpful in business to offer something that is fantastic in a literal sense – beyond reality. It can backfire big-time when they actually fail to deliver. The client regrets that he rashly accepted such an impossible offer.

Choices

- The client says yes, accepting what the supplier says he can do at face value.
- The client asks the supplier to show him how he proposes to fulfil the order.
- The client hesitates and allows the supplier to have second thoughts.

Decisions

The client accepts what he thinks is a fantastic deal and awaits delivery. On the appointed day, the supplier fails to deliver the order. The client can't understand why. He has the documentation to prove when the order was made. At no stage did the supplier hint that there was any problem. On reflection the client realizes that at the time he did feel the whole deal was too good to be true. He now has a problem; how to get the order fulfilled by someone who obviously cannot be trusted.

The supplier offers a fabulous deal at an incredible price. The client can't believe his luck. But before he signs up, he asks the supplier to show him how he can possibly make such a deal. The client has a suspicion that the supplier may not be able to do what he's promised. If he can obtain written confirmation on how the deal is to go ahead, he may be reassured. At least the client can save himself from a possible pitfall. If the supplier is unrealistic, there is no need for the client to behave foolishly as well.

On hearing about the fantastic offer, the client hesitates. He may be naturally sceptical or he may have been caught out with people who over-promise and under-deliver before. The supplier wants to win, or be liked, so he says he can do something even though he knows he cannot. By hesitating the client retains control of the situation. He allows the supplier time to rethink and perhaps adjust his unrealistic offer yet still secure the order.

Outcomes

The client who takes the supplier's words at face value should know better. It is easy to accept unrealistic offers if the terms are particularly attractive, but sometimes it pays to check. His desire to secure a great deal will prove costly in the end. If he asks the supplier for confirmation of the deal, so that he has documentary proof of what is being offered, he at least may save himself the trouble of being left without any goods having already paid for them. It is wise to test the veracity of the salesperson as soon as possible. Having second thoughts is always sensible. The client feels instinctively that what is on offer can't be true. He hesitates and allows the supplier to reflect on what he's just promised. Some people want to be helpful but it won't be in anyone's interests if the end result will be failure to produce the order because the terms are unrealistic.

Conclusion

Some people just want to be helpful and please others. Despite the difficulties, they will say that they can do the impossible, and unfortunately others believe them. They may feel it is weak to say they cannot do something. But nothing is gained by over-promising and failing to deliver. The supplier who is so keen to get an order that he promises the impossible must be feeling extremely insecure and anxious. If he is given some breathing space by the client he may think sensibly and realize that he'd better reconsider his rash offer. Being honest will not necessarily lose him the client; being unrealistic probably will.

Over-friendly colleagues who are irresistibly charming. How to say 'No' to unwanted requests from a wily individual

SITUATION

Popularity at work is something to be aimed for. But the colleague who chats to everyone and gets on first name terms at the earliest opportunity is a force to be reckoned with. He is so friendly, it's almost unnerving. What do charmers want? Usually they have a purpose and that is to make other colleagues behave like putty in their hands. They are clever about getting their own way by being so nice to people that they don't suspect he is up to tricks and can't help falling in with their wishes. Charmers don't consider that their demands and interruptions are a nuisance because they take such pains to be pleasant to everyone.

The office charmer invites a colleague to attend a conference in his place. He explains that 'there's no one who could fill my shoes better than you. I know you'll have a great time and meet lots of interesting people.' The colleague doesn't have the desire or the time to go, so how should he refuse such a polite request?

Choices

- The colleague wishes he could say 'No'. He thanks the charmer for thinking of him, and accepts the invitation. He attends the conference even though it is of limited value and he can't afford time away from the office.

- At the first opportunity, the colleague cuts the charmer short. He says he can't cope with the interruption; he doesn't want to accept whatever it is that's on offer. He explains that he's realized it is usually for the benefit of the charmer and not the person who's on the receiving end. He asks him to accept his refusal now and in the future.

- The colleague says that it is very kind to offer him the chance to go to the conference. It is something he would have loved to do only he has several important meetings and appointments over that period of time which commit him to staying in the office.

- The charmer is given a polite refusal from his colleague who suggests the names of a couple of other members of the company. The colleague assures the charmer that either of these persons would not only be better qualified than he but also, from the positions they occupy within the organization, more suited to attend the conference.

Decisions

Accepting what the charmer has offered is capitulating fully with his wily scheme. The conference is probably a complete time-waster; this is why the charmer doesn't want to attend himself. Yet someone from the company has to go. He picks his 'victim' and ingratiates himself to such an extent that the colleague takes the line of least resistance and agrees to fall in with his plans. The colleague wishes he had not accepted, because he knows the charmer regards him as a 'pushover' and will not hesitate to put other things on to him at a future date.

The colleague has grown wary of the charmer and decides to make a stand. He tells the charmer what he feels, resulting in the charmer being surprised by his attitude. He retires hurt, but wastes no time in spreading news throughout the company that a particular colleague must be under stress and struggling since he has behaved so unreasonably towards him. The colleague may have made a dangerous enemy in the charmer. He will turn the tables on the person who stood up to him by charming other colleagues against him.

The charmer's offer is refused, politely and effectively by his colleague. The colleague's schedule that prevents him attending the conference may be embellished or it may be true. The charmer has no choice but to accept his colleague's word at face value and move on to his next quarry.

The colleague who parries the charmer's offer with an alternative suggestion is being clever. He is using the same tactics shown by the charmer and turning the tables on him. He is polite, possibly even flattering to the charmer, when he thanks him profusely for thinking of him. However, he says he is not the most appropriate person for the task and suggests a couple of other names of individuals who could fill the role. The charmer realizes he has met his match.

Outcomes

The colleague who accepted the charmer's invitation to attend the conference was laying himself open for future assaults. He realized his weak response was the wrong decision but hadn't the foresight to come up with any resistance. The outright refusal to the charmer by the impatient colleague was an honest but possibly an unwise move. Oleaginous types of people, like this charmer, have the ability to twist things to their own advantage. The direct-speaking colleague has laid up potential trouble for himself and may be at risk in future from barbed insults instigated by the charmer, but never seen directly coming from his lips. The colleague who 'had plans' made a good stand against the charmer. It was not easy for the charmer to brush his reasons aside. In any case the charmer doesn't waste time with people who give plausible resistance. He would rather move on to an easier target. The colleague who played the charmer at his own game was a worthy opponent. There was nothing for the charmer to do but accept defeat and move on. He will think twice before approaching that colleague again to dump some other unwanted task on his desk.

Conclusion

Dealing with charming but wily characters requires emotional intelligence and a degree of courage. Saying 'No' isn't always easy and it is particularly difficult when faced with someone who is charming but grimly determined to get his own way. The best advice is to practise saying no to people whenever appropriate – the more it is done the easier it gets.

Chapter 11
The importance of emotional intelligence in the world of social media and mobile communications
... and the law of unintended consequences

The world wide web has created a 'global village' where everyone can potentially know everyone else's business. Its impact is immediate and it can be a force for both good and evil.

On a large scale, social media can foment revolutions and help topple governments. At a personal level it can build or destroy reputations, create enduring relationships or just cause embarrassment if not used wisely.

Companies such as Apple have reinvented themselves and been hugely successful as universal suppliers of web-enabled musical and other content. Google can show the world your house and even tell us what's going on inside it.

Advancement in technology is progressively changing the way that people and organizations can communicate and is continuing to do so at a staggering rate. Whereas people used to buy programs to run on their personal computers, through what is now known as the 'Cloud', they can now use programs and information that permanently reside on the internet and not their PCs. Not only is this more efficient but it also provides access to facilities that might otherwise be unavailable and unaffordable.

Such is the power of communications technology; the implications for 'what' we communicate provide new and important challenges to our emotional intelligence.

A simple guide to making emotionally intelligent 'netiquette' decisions

Do you have 'a face for radio'?

Facebook, as its name suggests, is the place where your face makes the first impression on others – unless, that is, you have substituted your face with something more cryptic. It is worth being circumspect about the pictures you put on social network sites as people form instant opinions on what they see. If, for example, you were applying for a job, the chances these days are that your potential employer would check you out using some form of new media. If pictures you have posted on social media sites show you in a drunken or irresponsible state, they will do you no favours – however capable or responsible you may be when sober! The key is to present yourself at all times for all audiences not just your immediate circle of friends, acquaintances and colleagues who will be familiar with your virtues.

Do you punctuate with expletives?

In a similar way to your face, your language will reveal things about you that you might not want everyone to know. After all, the basis of emotional intelligence is the understanding of not just your own emotional framework but also that of others. Some people are not offended by expletives while others form an instant opinion, which, of course, may be unfounded. Emotional intelligence is about taking the wider, longer view of likely effects over time. It is a shame when people prejudice their future because they are not taking account of all the contexts in which their communication will be judged.

Be careful who you tell

Although it provides a very quick and convenient way of telling your friends, posting details of your upcoming celebration, party or visit will notify a much wider audience and there may well be unintended consequences. There have been various press reports of hundreds of gatecrashers at small, domestic parties trashing premises, causing violence and involving the police. Every time you make an announcement it could be in the public domain and prey to unwanted response unless you have taken specific steps to protect your privacy such as that available through Facebook, Twitter and other social media companies.

Inappropriate publicity

There is a very real chance that if you have recorded it digitally, others will get hold of it and may use it in ways that you had never intended. Given that, these days, passing strangers can log into what you thought was a private network, information recorded digitally may be more vulnerable than some people would expect. Unless you have a good knowledge of file and network protection systems you cannot always be sure how effectively you are protecting your privacy. There are many examples of celebrities' inappropriate videos being publicized worldwide, satisfying some prurient needs, maybe, but ruining reputations. Of course, on the principle that 'it is better to be hated than ignored', some have allowed material into the public domain and you can argue that, from an emotional intelligence perspective, they have manipulated the situation to keep themselves prominent for longer – but some might say that was a cynical view.

Recent examples of a well-followed individual on Twitter show that audiences of millions could actively read a 'tweet' on the same day it is published. If that tweet was uncontrolled – and many are – it can spread biased or unsubstantiated information on a colossal scale, and effectively distort reality.

Boasting may impress you but does it impress others?

Because you can promote yourself and your opinions to an unlimited audience, there is sometimes a temptation to concentrate more on what you say about yourself and what you do than what is of genuine interest to others. Self-indulgence is, generally speaking, less emotionally intelligent than indulging your audience. This applies to you as an individual and also to the products or services that your organization may be wishing to promote. The internet is an exceptionally powerful tool but its power is no substitute for intelligent calculation of likely consequences.

How to obscure understanding

There is a natural tendency in businesses and the professions to develop their own language, jargon or acronyms. Although this may be convenient shorthand for those who work in these environments, it creates a 'them and us' culture as perceived by an outsider.

Also, but not necessarily deliberate, are different linguistic habits across the generations.

Some people deliberately use jargon to give themselves ascendancy over those who may not understand it. Although it may temporarily elevate their status, in the long term it shows the lack of confidence that their language is aiming, consciously or otherwise, to disguise.

In the context of new media, the language of social groupings will have an impact on whether the group wants to remain exclusive or become wider and more inclusive. It is neither right nor wrong but a mechanism designed to achieve specific aims. It would not be emotionally intelligent to aim for inclusiveness yet practise an exclusive way of communicating.

Beware what you send to friends

Some people are careless and some are fickle. It is very easy to send or forward information you would like to share with your friends. The danger is that they will innocently, but sometimes indiscreetly send that information to their friends too. The trouble is that their friends might not be your friends.

Many people have been acutely embarrassed by information reaching the wrong hands – resulting in lawsuits, divorces, feuds, blackmail and even assault.

Whereas word of mouth may be comparatively innocuous, electronic communication provides definitive and even alterable evidence of your words and thinking. If in doubt, don't send it.

EQ, new media and marketing

Social media present huge marketing opportunities (as evidenced by the new media billionaires so often in the news) but things can very easily go wrong. As social media deal so much with sentiment and opinion, it is very easy to get a distorted view of the truth, whether positive or negative, and for others to 'follow' that opinion as if it were fact.

There is a saying that if politicians receive seven letters on the same topic, they think it must be a campaign. It is thus possible for an unrepresentative sample to be seen as a majority view.

In using new media for marketing, it is therefore essential to anticipate any negative publicity and outweigh it with positive publicity so that any negatives are seen as unrepresentative. Techniques to achieve this are now widely practised, particularly in the area of product reviews or where individuals want to build reputations before others can spoil them. As a for instance, some people now seek multiple recommendations on social media sites so as to maximize their attractiveness to potential employers – before a current or previous employer or colleague can undermine that position.

Perception is more important than reality

Rules of intelligent decision-making and communication apply to new media as much as they apply to any other medium. The difference is in the size of the worldwide online community, the speed with which information is made available and the fact that information can be retained indefinitely in places you may never know about. It's like pressing the accelerator pedal for the first time in a very fast car. Before doing so make certain you know how the brakes work. In essence, you can get into trouble much faster if you are using such a powerful engine.

If you are emotionally intelligent, you will be fully aware that all others may not be so. This means that you must manage their perceptions. This involves a degree of positive manipulation, an understanding of the psychology of effective communication and a judicious choice of what you show and say to your audience.

With new media, you cannot afford to be too spontaneous. You should have taken account of all likely reactions and considered your best route to the most positive outcomes given your own and the recipients' circumstances. You have many choices to make, but there is an opportunity for spectacular results when you get things right.

Chapter 12
Measuring your emotional intelligence

There are many tests that purport to measure your EQ. However, because so much of emotional intelligence depends on how you might react to different circumstances and take random sets of variables into account, none can be considered totally definitive on its own – despite some beliefs to the contrary.

It is, however, possible to address individual topics or groupings of topics that will give you clear and reliable indicators in specific areas. As stated previously, whether you were to score high or low in such tests would not necessarily be a representation of your worth but simply how you are and the areas of EQ that you (or others) could potentially develop.

Some people focus emotional intelligence measurement on performance development and others on character building. Some tests aim to measure both.

What is your capacity for objective thought?

To be as effective as you can as a human being, you need to have an understanding of self *and* others. As people are not necessarily what their words and behaviour represent, a key component in demonstrating higher EQ is the capacity for objective thought – stepping outside your own experiences and pre-judgements to consider the underlying truths in any situation. This is not necessarily easy as we all have our distinctive temperaments, backgrounds, hidden agendas and different degrees of self-control. It is an aptitude, however, that we can grow.

Taking both personality characteristics and practical ability into account, there are certain basic characteristics that would merit better understanding in assessing your own and others' emotional framework. These indicate our ability to overcome challenges and interact with others. They include:

1 Clarity of (personal and/or organizational) goals

2 Positive as compared to negative values/attitudes

3 Competent self-management

4 Self-control

5 Orientation to personal development

6 Orientation to own and others' well-being

7 Capacity for objective thought

8 Self-esteem

9 Motivation

10 Commitment

11 Interpersonal awareness

12 Sociability

13 Collaborative ability

14 Decision-making skills

15 Adaptability

16 Imagination (as compared to knowledge)

17 Ability to structure and plan

Below is a set of questions designed to test your perception of your own emotional intelligence and a range of scores to show how you might rate yourself from an EQ perspective. It is based on your self-perception and should ideally be compared with an equivalent 360-degree input from friends, family and/or a range of colleagues to increase its validity. Because we are dealing with the subject of emotion, the questions cover what you feel and perceive as well as what you know. In the end, if you have been objective, you will be the best judge of how emotionally intelligent you are in the context of these questions. They will also highlight some areas where your EQ could be further developed.

(Health Warning: In the same way that it would be seen as a nightmare to get two sets of economists to agree with each other, and to come up with 100 per cent accurate forecasts, there are many unresolved controversies in the relatively new world of EQ. People must therefore make up their own minds about the effectiveness of the different tools used to measure emotional intelligence and the different interpretations they bring to bear.)

In answering each three-part (and one four-part) question in each table, please tick the relevant box to denote your score. 1 = the lower value and 5 = the higher for the purpose of this exercise, but no score is necessarily better or worse; it simply maps your style, orientation or likely behaviour. The aggregate scores will, however, give an overall emotional intelligence indicator and your 'stake in the ground' for further development. At the end of the test add the number of ticks in each of the five columns to reach a grand total for all 17 tables. This gives you a score out of 52 for each column.

TABLE 12.1   A test to show the positive aspects of your emotional intelligence

1.	To what extent do you personally act on specific goals and objectives you want to achieve within a specified time period:		1	2	3	4	5
		Short term?					
		Medium term?					
		Long term?					
		Total					
2.	When faced with challenging people and situations, how well do you believe you will:		1	2	3	4	5
		Overcome challenges?					
		Cope with difficult people?					
		Master your feelings?					
		Total					
3.	How well do you manage the different aspects of your own work and life:		1	2	3	4	5
		Your activities?					
		Your personal resources?					
		Your relationships?					
		Total					
4.	Faced with situations where you are likely to react strongly, do you:		1	2	3	4	5
		Control anger well?					
		Resist being indifferent?					
		Avoid impetuous response?					
		Total					

TABLE 12.1 *Continued*

5.	To what extent are you:		1	2	3	4	5
		A curious person?					
		A keen/natural learner?					
		An ambitious person?					
		Total					
6.	When faced with challenges or making decisions, how important to you are:		1	2	3	4	5
		Your personal well-being?					
		The well-being of others?					
		The impact you can make?					
		Total					
7.	When appraising situations, people or individuals how far do you:		1	2	3	4	5
		Suspend initial judgement?					
		Seek further evidence?					
		Take in all salient factors?					
		Total					
8.	When needing to influence others, how far do you:		1	2	3	4	5
		Ask them questions?					
		Say what you want?					
		Believe you will succeed?					
		Total					

TABLE 12.1 *Continued*

			1	2	3	4	5
9.	Faced with a new challenge are you most likely to:						
		Welcome the opportunity?					
		Embrace the task?					
		Expect positive results?					
		Total					
10.	In a role where you or others stand to gain, how far do you:		1	2	3	4	5
		Get involved immediately?					
		Take initiative?					
		Complete what you started?					
		Total					
11.	When mixing with others in a work and/or social environment, to what extent do you:		1	2	3	4	5
		Gauge others' moods?					
		Gauge others' needs?					
		Gauge their intentions?					
		Total					
12.	When meeting with a new person or group of people, how far do you:		1	2	3	4	5
		Greet with enthusiasm?					
		Make them feel good?					
		Engage their interest?					
		Total					

TABLE 12.1 *Continued*

13.	When working with others towards a specific decision or outcome, do you:		1	2	3	4	5
		Avoid first judgement?					
		Reconcile differences?					
		Seek mutual benefit?					
		Total					
14.	In reaching a decision for yourself, do you:		1	2	3	4	5
		Take account of your own needs?					
		Consider others' needs?					
		Assess longer term effect?					
		Total					
15.	When the unexpected happens or something does not work out as intended, how far do you:		1	2	3	4	5
		Think of alternatives, fast?					
		Engage others' help?					
		Take decisive action?					
		Total					
16.	When contemplating an important change that might affect you and others, how far do you:		1	2	3	4	5
		Seek radical solutions?					
		Think 'outside the box'?					
		Permit the unthinkable?					
		Total					

TABLE 12.1 *Continued*

17.	Having decided on a particular course of action in a project, to what extent will you:		*1*	*2*	*3*	*4*	*5*
		Have a success measure?					
		Have a planned approach?					
		Secure your resources?					
		Manage the process well?					
		Total					
			1	*2*	*3*	*4*	*5*
		Grand Totals					

If in columns 4 and/or 5 your score is between 40 and 52 your emotional intelligence is evidently high.

If, in column 3, your score is over 30, there are clearly areas of your life and work where you have the potential to change and grow your life for the better.

If in columns 1 and/or 2 you have a score over 20, you would gain by displacing some of the ways you currently think and behave with an approach that would be more rewarding for both yourself and others.

NB: The questionnaire above only tests the positive, not the negative. In order to address negative or painful issues that improved emotional intelligence might resolve – such as lack of confidence, lack of direction, motivation and self-belief – it would be advisable to seek the support of someone qualified to help you reverse that situation.

A further test that can be revealing, provocative and fun!

Analogies can work very well in helping you model your state of mind and can reveal unconscious characteristics or situations that affect people.

The following, scenario-based exercise has both a serious and lighter side and is often used to stimulate conversation in a social as well as work context.

It is about a **walk in the woods** and asks the following:

1 You live in the woods. Think about where you live and describe it to me.

2 You walk down a path and on that path see a vase. Describe it to me. What, if anything, do you do with it?

3 You carry on walking down the path and you come across a wild animal. What is it and what is it doing?

4 You carry on walking and come to water. Describe the water. How do you cross the water?

5 Once across the other side of the water, you reach a wall. What sort of wall is it and, if you can see over it (maybe you can't), what do you see on the other side?

In considering the answers, and discussing them, take into account the points on page 234.

A corporate tool

EQ measurement is being increasingly used in recruitment and performance-improvement programmes, management development, business communication, sales and other aspects of business life. There are many different models, so it is worth investigating in detail if you would like to apply them for yourself. The only caveat is to apply emotional intelligence to your choice!

1 Question 1 will describe home life and circumstances. If you only describe the house but do not refer to or indicate your home life, not everything in your home life may be as it should be. If the place you live is surrounded by woods and trees, you may well be surrounded by people you care about. If trees are not mentioned, then you are probably not.

2 The vase represents aspects of your career. The more ornate the vase, the more you are into your career. What you do with the vase indicates how opportunistic you are.

3 The animal represents your fears. How you pass the animal reflects how you deal with your fears.

4 If the water is deep, you have deep emotional feelings for your partner or spouse. If the water is shallow, there are fewer emotional ties. If the water is turbulent then so could be the relationship. How you cross the water shows how you handle your relationships.

5 The wall represents your future. If you can look over the wall, what you see is how you envisage life ahead. If the wall is too high, you may be frightened by your future.

Index